Guide to the

Wales Coast Path: **Pembrokeshire**

Cardigan to Amroth

Abereiddy and the 'Blue Lagoon'

www.walescoastpath.gov.uk | www.walescoastpath.co.uk

Guide to the
Wales Coast Path
Pembrokeshire

Cardigan to Amroth

*186 miles/ 300 kilometres of
superb coastal walking*

Vivienne Crow

Northern Eye
Books

www.northerneyebooks.co.uk

Text: Vivienne Crow

Series editor: Tony Bowerman

Introductory section: Tony Bowerman

Photographs: © Crown copyright (2015) Visit Wales, Drew Buckley/ www.drewbuckleyphotography.com, David Evans/ www.pemcoastphotos.com, Vivienne Crow, Dennis Kelsall, Carl Rogers, Shutterstock, Dreamstime

Design: Carl Rogers

Northern Eye Books
ISBN **978-1-908632-23-4**

A CIP catalogue record for this book is available from the British Library

www.northerneyebooks.co.uk
www.walescoastpath.co.uk

Twitter: @WalesCoastUK
         @Northerneyeboo

Important Advice: The route described in this book is undertaken at the reader's own risk. Walkers should take into account their level of fitness, wear suitable footwear and clothing, and carry food and water. It is also advisable to take the relevant OS maps with you in case you get lost and leave the area covered by our maps.

Whilst every care has been taken to ensure the accuracy of the route directions, the publishers cannot accept responsibility for errors or omissions, or for changes in the details given. Nor can the publisher and copyright owners accept responsibility for any consequences arising from the use of this book.

If you find any inaccuracies in either the text or maps, please write or email us at the addresses below. Thank you.

Acknowledgements: Warm thanks are due to everyone who helped make this book a reality. Thank you, in particular, to Natural Resources Wales' officer Quentin Grimley, who has worked tirelessly on the Wales Coast Path since 2007, and who has been more than generous with his friendly advice and support. Thanks, too, to the Wales Coast Path officers for each local authority along the Path, tourism officers, museum and library staff, Wales on View picture researchers, freelance photographers, and everyone else who has played a part. And, finally, thanks to Dave Quarell, end-to-end walker, for his quote explaining why the Wales Coast Path is so special

First published in 2015 by

Northern Eye Books Limited
Tattenhall, Cheshire CH3 9PX

Email: tony@northerneyebooks.com

For trade and sales enquiries, please call
01928 723 744

Contents

Official Guides to the Wales Coast Path

The Official Guides to the Wales Coast Path are endorsed by **Natural Resources Wales,** the body responsible for coordinating the development of the route. The guides split the Path into seven main sections with a guide for each. Together, they cover the entire 870-mile Path from the outskirts of Chester in the north to Chepstow in the south.

For details of the full range of Official Guides to the Wales Coast Path, see: **www.walescoastpath.gov.uk/plan-your-trip/guidebooks.aspx**

Wales Coast Path
Discover the shape of a nation

Wales is the largest country in the world with a continuous path around its entire coast. The **Wales Coast Path** promises 870 miles/1400 kilometres of unbroken coastal walking, from the outskirts of Chester in the north to Chepstow in the south. Along the way you'll experience the best of Wales: stunning scenery, stirring history, Welsh culture, and wildlife in abundance. If you tackle only one big walk in your life, make it this one. It's unmissable.

Great Orme, North Wales

Bwa Gwyn, Anglesey

Pearl-bordered fritillary

Caernarfon Castle, Gwynedd

Bardsey Island, Llŷn

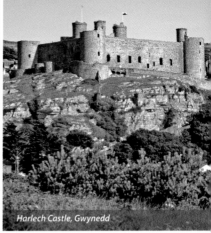
Harlech Castle, Gwynedd

Tenby, Pembrokeshire

Atlantic grey seal

Rhossili Bay, Gower

Millennium Centre, Cardiff

Wales Coast Path
An 870-mile coastal adventure

When the **Wales Coast Path** opened in May 2012, Wales became the largest country in the world with a continuous path around its entire coast. Walkers can now enjoy unparalleled coastal walking around the Welsh seaboard from top to bottom: from the outskirts of the ancient walled city of Chester, on the Dee Estuary in the north, to the pretty market town of Chepstow, on the Severn Estuary, in the southeast.

The official, signposted and waymarked path covers roughly 870 miles/1400 kilometres and starts and finishes within easy reach of the two ends of the historic 177 mile/285 kilometre Offa's Dyke National Trail. This means keen walkers can make a complete circumnavigation of Wales; a total distance of around 1,050 miles/1,685 kilometres. Ever keen for a new challenge, a few hardy walkers had already completed the full circuit within months of the Wales Coast Path's opening.

But whether you prefer to walk the whole coast path in one go, in occasional sections, or a few miles at a time, you're in for a real treat. There's

Skomer Island seen from Deer Park, Pembrokeshire

something new around every corner, and you'll discover places that can only be reached on foot. Visually stunning and rich in both history and wildlife, the coast path promises ever-changing views, soaring cliffs and spacious beaches, sea caves and arches, wildflowers, seabirds, seals and dolphins, as well as castles, cromlechs, coves and coastal pubs. It's a genuinely special landscape.

This visual and ecological richness is recognised nationally and internationally. In fact, the Wales Coast Path runs past 1 Marine Nature Reserve, 1 Geopark, 2 National Parks, 3 Areas of Outstanding Natural Beauty, 3 World Heritage Sites, 7 official and unofficial nudist beaches, 11 National Nature Reserves, 14 Heritage Coasts, 17 Special Protection Areas, 21 Special Areas of Conservation, 23 Historic Landscapes, 42 Blue Flag beaches and 111 marine Sites of Special Scientific Interest. Large stretches of coast are also managed and protected by Wildlife Trusts, the RSPB and the National Trust.

Long-distance walkers will enjoy the unbroken path, the solitude, the coast's constantly changing moods and the back-to-nature challenge. Holiday and weekend walkers can recharge their batteries, see something new, and regain an ever more necessary sense of perspective. Families can potter, play and explore. And locals can walk the dog, jog, get fit and rediscover their home patch. Whatever your preferences, the Wales Coast Path promises something for everyone.

"Walking around Wales was by far the most awe-inspiring, perspective-changing experience of my life."

Dave Quarrell,
First person to complete the Wales Coast Path and Offa's Dyke Path Nation Trail together, 2012

All or Part?

So, what's the best way to walk the Wales Coast Path? The 870 mile/1400 kilometre route covers the whole of the Welsh seaboard and is the longest and probably the best of all Britain's long-distance challenges.

But of course, not everyone has the time, energy or inclination to walk it all at once. Instead, most people start with a short stretch, discover they love it, and come back for more.

Section by section

1. North Wales Coast
2. Isle of Anglesey
3. Llŷn Peninsula
4. Cardigan Bay & Ceredigion
5. Pembrokeshire
6. Carmarthen Bay & Gower
7. South Wales Coast

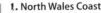

1. North Wales Coast

Chester to Bangor

80 miles/125 kilometres

7 Day Sections

Undulating coast. Vast Dee estuary, traditional seaside towns, limestone headland, and Conwy mountain

2. Isle of Anglesey

Circuit of island from Menai Bridge

125 miles/200 kilometres

12 Day Sections

Grand coastal scenery from tidal straits to bays, estuaries, dunes and cliffs. Area of Outstanding Natural Beauty

3. Llŷn Peninsula

Bangor to Porthmadog

110 miles/180 kilometres

9 Day Sections

Unspoilt peninsula with bays, coves and cliffs, tipped by Bardsey Island. Area of Outstanding Natural Beauty

4. Cardigan Bay & Ceredigion

Porthmadog to Cardigan

140 miles/225 kilometres

12 Day Sections

Low-lying dunes and big estuaries followed by steeper, grassy sea cliffs with dramatic coves and bays

5. Pembrokeshire

Cardigan to Amroth

186 miles/300 kilometres

14 Day Sections

Varied, beautiful, popular. The Pembrokeshire Coastal Path is a National Trail and coastal National Park

6. Carmarthen Bay & Gower

Tenby to Swansea

130 miles/210 kilometres

12 Day Sections

Long sandy beaches, tidal estuaries, dramatic rocky coast. Area of Outstanding Natural Beauty

7. South Wales Coast

Swansea to Chepstow

115 miles/185 kilometres

11 Day Sections

Traditional beach resorts, seafaring and industrial landscapes.

Heritage Coast, National Nature Reserves

Strait and narrow: *The Menai Strait separates Anglesey/Ynys Môn from the Welsh mainland*

Wales: Top to Bottom

Walking the whole 870 miles/1400 kilometres of the Wales Coast Path in one go is an increasingly popular challenge. Some people have even run all the way. By a curious coincidence, the overall distance is almost exactly the same as Britain's famous top-to-bottom route, from John o' Groats to Land's End — a very long way.

The Wales Coast Path will take you from the outskirts of Chester, down the broad Dee estuary, along the North Wales coast with its traditional seaside resorts and impressive limestone headlands at Little and Great Orme, past Conwy Castle, over Conwy Mountain and on along the wooded Menai Strait. The path then loops around the rugged, offshore Isle of Anglesey, or Ynys Môn, passes the walled town of Caernarfon and its castle before heading around the remote Llŷn Peninsula with Bardsey Island balanced at its tip. From Criccieth and Porthmadog the path pushes south past Harlech Castle — kissing the western rim of the Snowdonia National Park — and on down the majestic sweep of Cardigan Bay with its beautiful, open estuaries. It then rounds Pembrokeshire — Britain's only coastal National Park — with

its sparkling bays and lofty cliffs. Striding through Carmarthenshire and crossing the wide Tywi and Tâf estuaries, the path curves around the lovely Gower Peninsula into Swansea Bay. Beyond the striking Glamorgan Heritage Coast, the path runs along the Cardiff Bay waterfront to Cardiff, the lively capital of Wales. From there, it's only a short stretch alongside the broad Severn Estuary to the pretty market town of Chepstow on the Welsh-English border and the southern end of the Wales Coast Path.

Only the fittest, most determined walkers can hope to complete the entire path in 6-7 weeks, averaging 20 or so miles a day.

At a more leisurely pace — allowing time to soak up the atmosphere and enjoy the views, and with regular pauses to watch the wildlife, swim, enjoy a quiet drink or visit some of the fascinating places along the way — you should allow around three months for the whole trip.

Remember, though, the Wales Coast Path is a challenging route with plenty of rough ground, narrow paths and ups-and-downs (an overall total ascent and descent of 95,800 feet/ 29,200 metres). There are tempting detours and places to see along the way, too. So it's perhaps best to plan slightly shorter and more realistic daily distances than you might ordinarily cover.

You should also allow extra time for the unexpected, to rest or to hole up in bad weather. As a rule of thumb, it's better to be ahead of schedule, with time to enjoy the experience, rather than always having to push ahead to reach the next overnight stop.

The Official Guidebooks in this series break the path down into seven main sections (see the map on page 10), each of which is then sub-divided into carefully-planned 'Day Sections' — usually averaging around 10-15 miles each. These typically start and finish either in, or near easy-to-reach towns, villages or settlements, many of them on bus routes, and with shops, pubs, restaurants, cafés and places to stay nearby.

No matter how long it takes, walking the whole of the Wales Coast Path is a real achievement. For most of us, it would be the walk of a lifetime.

Walking around Wales a bit at a time

Yet, understandably, most people don't want to walk the whole path in one go. Instead, they prefer to do it bit by bit, often over several years: during annual and bank holidays, over long weekends, or as the whim takes them. Done in this leisurely fashion, the walk becomes a project to ponder, plan, and take pleasure in.

South Stack lighthouse, on the rocky north-west tip of Anglesey

Maritime wildflowers: *Yellow hawksbit fringes the coast path on Holyhead Mountain, Anglesey*

A popular way to enjoy the path is to book a short holiday close to a section of the path, and do a series of day walks along the surrounding coast, returning to your base each night.

Some people like to catch a train (especially along the North Wales Coast), bus or taxi to the start of their day's walk and then walk back (see the information at the start of each Day Section).

Another approach is to drive to the end of your planned section and then get a pre-booked local taxi to take you back to the start; this costs only a few pounds and lets you walk in one direction at your own pace.

If you're planning to walk a section over several days before returning to your starting point by bus or train, call Traveline on **0870 6082608** or visit **www.traveline-cymru.org.uk** for help with timetables and itineraries.

Best time to go?

Britain's main walking season runs from Easter to the end of September. Although the Wales Coast Path is delightful throughout the year, the best walking weather tends to be in late spring as well as early and late summer.

Although the Easter holiday is busy, spring is otherwise a quiet time of year. The days are lengthening and the weather getting steadily warmer.

Blessed isle: *Bardsey Island, or Ynys Enlli, has been the goal of seafarers and pilgrims since time immemorial*

Migrant birds and basking sharks are returning to Wales from farther south. The weather is also likely to be dry.

Early summer is ideal for walking. May and June enjoy the greatest number of sunshine hours per day (the average for May is 225 hours, and for June 210 hours) and the lowest rainfall of the year (average for May is 50mm, June is 51mm). You'll also have the accompaniment of a spectacular array of spring flowers and the chance to see breeding sea birds at their best.

High summer is the busiest season, particularly during the school holidays in July and August. Both the beaches and the Coast Path are likely to be packed in places. Finding somewhere to stay at short notice can be tricky, too — so it's best to book well in advance. However, the long sunny days are certainly attractive, and you can often walk in shorts and a T-shirt.

By September most visitors have returned home, and you'll have the path largely to yourself. The weather remains good and the sea is still warm enough for swimming. Sunny days often stretch into September, with the first of the winter storms arriving in late September and October. Autumn

also means the coastal trees and bracken are slowly turning from green to red, orange and gold.

Winter brings shorter, colder days with less sunlight and other disadvantages: unpredictable weather, stormy seas, high winds and even gales, along with closed cafés and accommodation. But for experienced walkers, the cooler days can bring peace and solitude and a heightened sense of adventure.

Welsh weather

Like the rest of Britain, Wales is warmed by the Gulf Stream's ocean current and enjoys a temperate climate. This is particularly true of the Llŷn Peninsula. Because Wales lies in the west of Britain, the weather is generally mild but damp. Low pressure fronts typically come in off the Irish Sea from the west and southwest, hitting the coast first and then moving inland to the east. This means rain and wet weather can occur at any time of year, so you should always take good waterproofs and spare clothes with you.

For more weather or a five-day forecast, visit **www.metoffice.com** or **www.bbc.co.uk/weather**. Several premium-rate national 'Weatherlines' give up-to-date forecasts, and the Snowdonia and Pembrokeshire National Parks websites provide local information, too.

Which direction?

The Official Guide books give directions from north to south, starting in Chester and ending in Chepstow. This means walkers will enjoy the sun on their faces for much of the way. Most luggage transfer services also run in this direction. Nonetheless, the path can be tackled in either direction. It's just easier to go with the flow.

Which section?

Choosing which part of the Wales Coast Path to walk depends in part on where you live, how long you've got and the kind of scenery you prefer.

Sections vary considerably. Arry Beresford-Webb, the first person to run the entire path in 2012 said, "I was stunned by the diversity of the path. Each section felt like I was going through a different country."

Some stretches are fairly wild, while others are more developed. Parts of the Isle of Anglesey, Llŷn Peninsula, Cardigan Bay and Pembrokeshire are often remote and away from large settlements. Other stretches, such as North Wales or the South Wales Coast around Swansea, Cardiff and Newport are busier, and often close to popular seaside towns or industry.

The terrain varies too. Much of the North Wales Coast is low-lying but punctuated with occasional headlands; as are much of Cardigan Bay, Carmarthen Bay and parts of the Glamorgan Heritage Coast.

In contrast, the Isle of Anglesey, Llŷn Peninsula, Pembrokeshire and Gower are often rocky with high sea cliffs, dramatic headlands, offshore islands and intimate coves.

Self sufficient or supported?

The other key decision for walkers is whether to arrange everything yourself or let someone else do it for you. For many people, devising their own itinerary and working out how to travel and where to stay is part of the fun. Others prefer to let one of the specialist walking holiday companies create the itinerary, book accommodation, arrange luggage transfers, meals and side trips. The main companies are listed at the back of the book.

Accommodation

There are plenty of places to stay within easy reach of the Wales Coast Path all around Wales. Most walkers either camp or stay in bed and breakfast accommodation; usually a mix of the two. There are plenty of hostels and bunkhouses along the way but, unfortunately, they are too unevenly spaced to provide accommodation every night.

Accommodation may be fully booked during peak holiday seasons, so it's advisable to book well ahead. Local Tourist Information Centres (TICs) will often know all the local accommodation providers, know who has vacancies, and can help with booking. For late, or emergency on-the-spot bookings, it's also worth contacting the TICs listed at the start of each Day Section.

Backpacking

Backpacking adds an extra dimension to the walking experience: being outdoors for days at a time, watching the sunrise and sunset, gazing at the stars overhead without artificial light getting in the way. But don't underestimate how much a heavy pack can slow you down. The secret is to travel as light as possible; the lightest tent or bivvy bag, a lightweight sleeping bag and waterproofs, and a single change of clothes.

There are plenty of official campsites along the busier sections of the Wales Coast Path. However, many are on small farms and may not advertise. Elsewhere campsites are often few and far between, and may need searching for. During peak season some may also be full, so it's advisable to book ahead. But remember, most sites are closed during the winter (typically from November to Easter, and often longer).

Unofficial 'wild camping' is a grey area. There is no legal right in England and Wales to 'wild camp' anywhere, including alongside the path. Every scrap of land in Britain belongs to someone, and many landowners frown on campers. So it makes sense to ask before pitching.

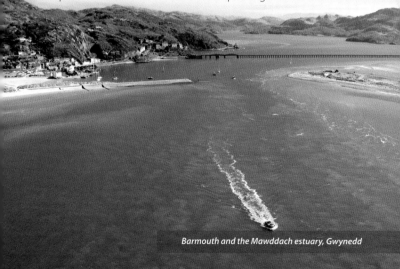

Barmouth and the Mawddach estuary, Gwynedd

Stile guide: *A walker on the Wales Coast Path with St Anne's Head, Pembrokeshire behind*

Unofficially, however, overnight camping is usually tolerated, so long as you pitch a small tent unobtrusively in the evening, and pack up and leave early the next morning, without leaving a trace.

Alternatively, there are popular luggage transfer services on the more established stretches of the path. For a small fee, they will pick up your rucksack and other bags and transport them to the end of your day's walk. A list of luggage transfer companies appears at the back of the book.

Clothes, boots and backpack

For those new to long-distance walking, it's worth emphasising the benefits of comfortable walking boots and suitable clothing. Walking continuously, day after day, puts extra pressures on your feet. Be prepared for changes in the weather, too. Carry waterproofs and remember that several thin layers allow you to adjust your clothing as conditions change.

Checking the weather forecast before you set off each day will help you decide what to wear. If you're in the car, it's worth taking a selection of clothing for different conditions, and deciding what to wear and carry immediately before you start.

Onshore breezes can mask the strength of the sun. To avoid sunburn, or even sunstroke, remember to slap on some sunscreen and wear a hat.

Other things to take, depending on weight, include: maps, water bottle, lightweight walking poles, basic First Aid including plasters and antiseptic cream, penknife, head torch and spare batteries, chocolate, sweets or energy bars, toilet paper, a small camera, binoculars, mobile phone, and a pen and notebook. Don't forget some spare cash too; most places accept cards but finding a Cashpoint or somewhere that offers 'Cash Back' near the path can be tricky.

Food and Drink

Although the Official Guides try to start and end each Day Section at places with amenities, some stretches are nonetheless remote and may have few places to buy food or drink. This may be the case for several days in a row. So it makes sense to plan ahead and carry enough supplies with you.

Conversely, other stretches are well supplied with shops, pubs, cafés, restaurants and takeaways; these are indicated at the start of each Day Section.

Coast Path Safety Code

- Take care on the Coast Path — it's rugged, natural terrain.
- Keep to the path, away from cliff edges and overhangs.
- Always supervise children, especially near cliff edges.
- Walking surfaces can vary considerably with the weather. Always wear strong footwear with a good grip and ankle support.
- Wear or carry warm and waterproof clothing.
- Cliff-top walking can be dangerous in high winds.
- Beware of taking shortcuts across beaches — you may be cut off by the tide. Swimming can also be dangerous.
- Do not sit under cliffs or climb them.
- Keep dogs under close control.
- The Coast Path is managed for walkers; it is not safe or lawful to ride horses or cycle along most of the Coast Path.
- Leave gates and property as you find them.

Maps

The maps in this book are reproduced to scale from the magenta-covered Ordnance Survey Landranger 1:50,000 series, enhanced with additional information. The official route of the Wales Coast Path is highlighted in orange. The numbers on the maps correspond to those in the route description for each Day Section.

Beautiful bay: *Walking on the Wales Coast Path above Porth Eynon, on Gower*

It's also worth taking the larger scale, orange-covered Ordnance Survey Explorer 1:25,000 maps with you. These show additional features such as Access Land, field boundaries, springs and wells.

Both scales of OS maps now have the official route of the Wales Coast Path marked on them as a line composed of a series of diamond symbols. Grid squares on both series of maps represent one square kilometre.

The relevant maps for each Day Section are listed at the beginning of each chapter. The grid references given in this book for the start and finish of each Day Section are from the Ordnance Survey maps.

Route finding

For the most part, the Wales Coast Path follows a single official route. In a few places, there are both official and unofficial alternative routes. Otherwise, the path hugs the coast as far is practically and legally possible, occasionally diverting inland around private estates, nature reserves, natural obstacles, estuaries, gunnery ranges and so on. The definitive route, and any occasional changes are notified on the official Wales Coast Path website.

The path uses a mixture of public rights of way: footpaths, bridleways and byways as well as lanes, open access land, beaches and some permissive paths. On most sections, the route is well-used and clear. In remote or under-used areas, however, walkers will need to pay closer attention to the maps and directions in this book.

Fingerposts and waymarkers

The Wales Coast Path is clearly signed and waymarked with its own distinctive logo: a white dragon-tailed seashell on a blue background surrounded by a yellow circlet bearing the words *'Llwybr Arfordir Cymru - Wales Coast Path'*. Look for the wood or metal fingerposts at main access points, in towns, on roadsides and lanes, and at key junctions.

Elsewhere, the route is clearly waymarked with plastic roundels fixed to stiles, gateposts, fences and walls. In many places the Wales Coast Path waymarkers sit alongside others for already established routes — such as the Pembrokeshire Coast Path National Trail or the Isle of Anglesey Coastal Path. In some areas these local waymarkers are still more in evidence than the official Wales Coast Path ones; and on some stretches, waymarking remains patchy.

Llansteffan Castle overlooks the sands of the Tywi Estuary, Carmarthenshire

Alternative routes

Two sorts of alternative route are described in the guides. The first are the **official alternative routes** that avoid remote or challenging sections; and more attractive routes that, for example, provide better views or get farther away from motor traffic.

The second are our own **unofficial alternative routes**. Many of these are beach routes below the high water mark that by their nature are not permanently available, and so do not qualify as part of the 'official route'. Both the **official** and **unofficial alternative routes** are shown on the maps in this book as a broken orange highlight.

Detours

The directions also describe **detours** to places of interest that we think you won't want to miss. These are usually short, off the main path, there-and-back routes, typically of no more than a kilometre or so in each direction. Suggested detours can take you to anything from a special pub, castle or church to a stunning view or waterfall. If you've got the time, they bring

Official route waymarkers *Official alternative route waymarker*

an extra dimension to the walk. Detours are shown on the maps as a blue broken highlight.

Temporary diversions

There may be occasional or seasonal temporary inland diversions. The reasons for them vary from land management and public safety: forestry work, cliff falls, landslips and floods, to wildlife conservation: protecting seal breeding sites, bird roosts and nesting sites, and so on. Details of the latest permanent and temporary diversions can be found on the official Wales Coast Path website under 'Route Changes'.

Tides and tide tables

As much as five percent of the Wales Coast Path runs along the foreshore, between mean high and low water. These sections are naturally affected

Clear waymarking: *Signs and waymarkers for the Pembrokeshire Coast Path National Trail and the Wales Coast Path often sit happily side-by-side*

by the tide. On the whole, the official Wales Coast Path avoids beaches and estuaries. However, beaches often provide time-honoured, direct and pleasant walking routes and are usually safely accessible, except for around 1½ hours either side of high tide. If the tide is in, or you're in any doubt, take the inland route instead.

Occasional streams and tidal creeks may also be crossed at low tide but be impassable at high water. So it is a good idea to carry tide tables with you and consult them before you set out each day. They are widely available for around £1 from coastal TICs, shops and newsagents.

Several websites also give accurate tidal predictions for locations around the UK, including downloadable five-day predictions. Useful websites include: **www.bbc.co.uk/weather/coast_and_sea/tide_tables** and **www.easytide.ukho.gov.uk**.

Safety advice

If you're new to long-distance walking, or in one of the remoter areas, please remember:

• Wear walking boots and warm, waterproof clothing.

• Take food and drink.

Layered limestone: *Nash Point on the Glamorgan Heritage Coast, South Wales*

- Mobile signals are patchy along much of the path; let someone know where you are heading and when you expect to arrive.
- If you decide to walk along a beach, always check tide tables.
- Stay on the path and away from cliff edges.
- Take extra care in windy and/or wet conditions.
- Always supervise children and dogs.
- Follow local signs and diversions.

Emergencies

In an emergency, call 999 or 112 and ask for the service your require: Ambulance, Police, Fire or Coastguard.

Tell them your location as accurately as possible (give an OS grid reference, if possible; and look for named landmarks), how many people are in your party, and the nature of the problem.

Remember, though, that mobile signals may be poor or absent in some areas. Some coastal car parks and main beach access points have emergency telephones. Coastal pubs and shops may also have phones you can ask to use in an emergency.

Who manages the coast path?

The Wales Coast Path is co-ordinated at a national level by Natural Resources Wales and managed on the ground by the sixteen local authorities and two National Parks through which it passes.

Funding has come from the Welsh Government, the European Regional Development Fund and the local authorities themselves.

For more details, see: **www.naturalresourceswales.gov.uk**

The Best of **Pembrokeshire**

The spectacular cliffs and beautiful beaches of Pembrokeshire offer some of the best coastal walking in the whole of Britain. With the underlying geology changing every few miles, the scenery is truly spectacular — as well as varied. Watch for natural arches, wave-cut platforms and drowned valleys as well as a wealth of wildlife, including seabirds, puffins, choughs, seals, dolphins and wildflowers. Every tiny cove, every settlement and every headland on this southwestern tip of Wales has a long and fascinating history, with the coast path passing Neolithic burial chambers, Iron Age forts, medieval castles and sites associated with the Celtic saints.

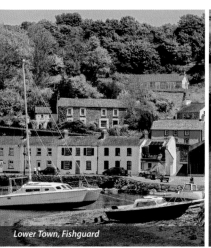

Lower Town, Fishguard

Strumble Head

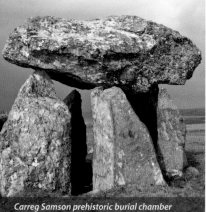

Carreg Samson prehistoric burial chamber

Blue Lagoon, near Abereiddy

St Davids Cathedral

Solva

Pembroke Castle

'Green Bridge of Wales'

Barafundle Bay

Tenby harbour

Pembrokeshire
Part of the **Wales Coast Path**

The dramatic Pembrokeshire coast is a dream destination for walkers: for 300 breathtaking kilometres, the National Trail winds its way along the top of rugged cliffs, in and out of secluded inlets and along seemingly endless beaches. From the remotest reaches of the north coast on day one to the popular beaches around Tenby on the final day, it provides a wonderfully varied experience. Whether you come for the scenery, the wildlife, the history or simply to immerse yourself in an exceptional corner of Britain, you won't be disappointed by Pembrokeshire.

*"To reach a port we must set sail,
Sail, not tie at anchor,
Sail, not drift."*

Franklin D. Roosevelt

The unique qualities of this special place were recognised in 1952 when it was designated as one of Britain's first National Parks. The Park includes several Sites of Special Scientific Interest, a National Nature Reserve and one of the UK's four Marine Nature Reserves, all helping to protect the area's wildlife, its habitats and its geology. In addition, several sections of the coast are managed by the National Trust.

Starting at St Dogmael's, the first few days of the Pembrokeshire Coast Path run along the county's rugged north coast with its high, often remote sections of windswept cliffs, dropping in on the towns of Newport, Fishguard and, just off route, the tiny cathedral city of St Davids. As the route rounds St Davids peninsula, it enters St Bride's Bay, home to numerous coves, beaches and historic headlands. Beyond the Marloes peninsula and then St Ann's Head, the nature of the coast path changes again as the more developed coast around the Milford Haven waterway beckons. Rounding the Angle peninsula, the path turns its back on these larger settlements and passes through spectacular limestone and red sandstone scenery on its way to lovely Tenby and its end point at Amroth Castle. All in all, it should take about a fortnight to complete — 14 days that promise an experience walkers won't forget.

Spring gorse frames a distant view of Strumble Head lighthouse

Walking the Pembrokeshire coast

The Pembrokeshire Coast Path runs for 186 miles / 300 kilometres between Cardigan, on the Ceredigion border, and Amroth Castle on the county border with Carmarthenshire. This guide splits the route into 14 convenient day sections, each of about 10-17 miles / 16-27 kilometres. Most of these start and finish in towns or villages with decent facilities for eating, sleeping and buying provisions. However, due to the remote nature of some sections, if

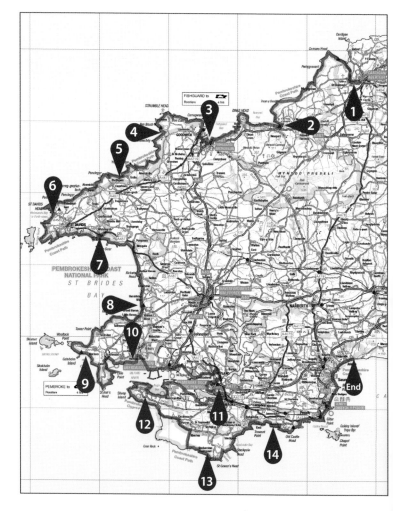

Day Section	Distance	Start	Finish
Day Section 1 Cardigan to Newport	17 miles 27Km	Cardigan SN 177 458	Newport SN 062 394
Day Section 2 Newport to Fishguard	11 miles 18Km	Newport SN 062 394	Fishguard SM 962 371
Day Section 3 Fishguard to Pwll Deri	10½ miles 17Km	Fishguard SM 962 371	Pwll Deri (YHA) SM 892 387
Day Section 4 Pwll Deri to Aber Draw	10 miles 16Km	Pwll Deri (YHA) SM 892 387	Aber Draw SM 834 324
Day Section 5 Aber Draw to Whitesands Bay	11 miles 18Km	Aber Draw SM 834 324	Whitesands Bay SM 734 271
Day Section 6 Whitesands Bay to Solva	13 miles 21Km	Whitesands Bay SM 734 271	Solva harbour SM 805 243
Day Section 7 Solva to Broad Haven	11 miles 18Km	Solva harbour SM 805 243	Broad Haven SM 861 138
Day Section 8 Broad Haven to Marloes Sands	12½ miles 20Km	Broad Haven SM 861 138	Marloes Sands SM 781 076
Day Section 9 Marloes Sands to Sandy Haven	13½ miles 21Km	Marloes Sands SM 781 076	Sandy Haven SM 853 075
Day Section 10 Sandy Haven to Pembroke	17 miles 27Km	Sandy Haven SM 853 075	Pembroke SM 983 016
Day Section 11 Pembroke to Angle	11 miles 18Km	Pembroke SM 983 016	Angle SM 866 028
Day Section 12 Angle to St Govan's Chapel	17 miles 27Km	Angle SM 866 028	St Govan's SR 966 930
Day Section 13 St Govan's Chapel to Manorbier	11 miles 17Km	St Govan's SR 966 028	Manorbier Bay SS 060 976
Day Section 14 Manorbier to Amroth Castle	15 miles 25Km	Manorbier Bay SS 060 976	Amroth SN 171 072

you aren't camping or staying in hostels, you may need to catch a bus or take a short walk inland to the nearest settlement. All the Day Sections are shown on the chart above.

Distance chart for key locations along the path

Miles (upper-right of diagonal) / *Kilometres* (lower-left of diagonal)

From \ To	Amroth	Saundersfoot	Tenby	Manorbier	St Govan's Chapel	Freshwater West	Angle	Pembroke	Milford Haven	Dale	Martin's Haven	St Bride's Haven	Broad Haven	Newgale	Solva	Porth Clais	Whitesands Bay	Abereiddy	Abercastle	Strumble Head	Fishguard	Newport	St Dogmaels	Cardigan
Cardigan	180	177	173	165	155	146	138	127	115	105	94	90	84	77	73	67	60	53	46	37	29	17	2	
St Dogmaels	178	175	171	163	153	144	136	125	113	103	93	88	82	75	71	65	58	51	44	35	27	16		3
Newport	163	160	155	148	137	129	121	109	98	87	77	73	66	60	55	49	43	35	29	19	11		25	28
Fishguard	152	149	144	137	127	118	109	98	86	76	66	62	55	49	44	38	32	24	18	8		18	43	46
Strumble Head	143	140	136	129	118	110	101	90	78	68	58	53	47	40	36	30	23	16	9		13	31	56	59
Abercastle	134	131	126	119	109	100	92	80	69	58	48	44	38	31	27	21	14	7		15	28	46	71	74
Abereiddy	128	124	120	113	102	94	85	74	62	52	42	37	31	25	20	14	7		10	26	39	57	82	85
Whitesands Bay	120	117	113	105	95	86	78	67	55	44	34	30	24	17	13	7		12	22	38	51	69	94	97
Porth Clais	113	110	106	98	88	79	71	60	48	38	28	23	17	10	6		11	23	33	48	62	80	105	108
Solva	107	104	100	92	82	73	65	54	42	32	22	17	11	4		10	21	33	43	58	71	89	114	117
Newgale	103	100	96	88	78	69	61	49	38	27	17	13	7		7	17	27	40	50	65	78	96	121	124
Broad Haven	96	93	89	82	71	63	54	43	31	21	11	6		11	18	27	38	50	61	76	89	107	132	135
St Bride's Haven	90	87	83	75	65	56	48	37	25	14	4		10	21	27	37	48	60	71	86	98	117	142	145
Martin's Haven	86	83	78	71	61	52	44	33	21	11		6	16	27	35	44	55	67	78	93	106	124	148	151
Dale	76	73	68	61	50	42	34	22	11		16	23	33	44	51	61	71	84	94	109	122	140	165	168
Milford Haven	65	62	58	50	40	31	23	12		17	33	40	50	61	68	78	88	100	111	126	139	157	182	185
Pembroke	53	50	46	39	28	20	11		19	36	52	59	69	80	86	96	107	119	129	145	158	176	201	204
Angle	42	39	35	27	17	8		18	37	54	70	77	87	98	105	115	125	137	148	163	176	194	219	222
Freshwater West	34	31	26	19	9		13	32	50	67	83	91	101	111	118	128	139	151	161	176	190	207	232	236
St Govan's Chapel	25	22	18	11		14	27	45	64	81	97	104	114	125	132	142	149	159	170	181	192	207	220	249
Manorbier	15	12	7		17	31	44	62	81	98	114	121	131	142	149	159	170	181	192	207	220	238	263	266
Tenby	7	4		12	29	42	56	74	93	110	117	126	133	143	154	161	170	181	193	204	219	232	250	275
Saundersfoot	3		7	19	36	54	63	81	100	117	133	138	150	155	166	173	188	200	211	226	239	257	282	285
Amroth		5	12	24	41	54	68	86	105	122	138	145	155	166	173	182	193	205	215	231	244	262	287	290

Distances are approximate to the nearest mile/kilometre

Wild coastline: *Strumble Head lighthouse framed by yellow, clifftop gorse*

Day Sections

1: Cardigan to Newport

Distance: 17 miles/ 27 kilometres

Terrain: Tough, exposed cliff-top walking with lots of ascent and descent involved. Rugged, remote section of coastline with no facilities en route

Points of interest: St Dogmael's Abbey; dramatic cliffs, stacks, arches and other geological features, including the Witches' Cauldron; lime kilns; Pen yr Afr, highest point on Pembrokeshire Coast Path; choughs and seabirds

Note: Accommodation and other facilities in St Dogmael's and Newport, but no amenities at all between the seasonal cafés at Poppit Sands and Newport Sands

2: Newport to Fishguard (Lower Town)

Distance: 11 miles/ 18 kilometres

Terrain: Cliff-top walking; not as high or exposed as previous day, but still lots of ups and downs. The climb to Dinas Head (142 metres) can be missed out

Points of interest: Attractive town of Newport; church ruins at Cwm-Yr-Eglwys; views from Dinas Head; choughs and seabird colonies; rugged cliff scenery; wildlife in Cwm Dewi meltwater channel; Fishguard fort; pretty harbour at Lower Town

Note: Wide range of accommodation and other facilities in Fishguard as well as campsites en route; historic pub at Pwllgwaelod near Dinas Island

3: Fishguard (Lower Town) to Pwll Deri

Distance: 10½ miles/ 17 kilometres

Terrain: Surfaced paths and roads along edge of Fishguard and through Goodwick; remote section of cliff-top, much of it heathland; less ascent and descent than on previous days

Points of interest: Ferry terminal at Fishguard; Garn Wen burial chamber; basalt columns on Pen Anglas; Carreg Goffa memorial; pillow lava at Strumble Head; birds and wildflowers on heathland; seals, porpoises and dolphins around Strumble Head

Note: Good facilities in Fishguard and Goodwick, but then nothing apart from the youth hostel at Pwll Deri. Stock up on provisions in Goodwick, because there are no dining facilities until Trefin at the end of section four and no shops until St David's at the end of section five

4: Pwll Deri to Aber Draw/Trefin

Distance: 10 miles/ 16 kilometres

Terrain: Airy ridge to start the day, rocky underfoot, then straightforward cliff-top paths; a few pebbly beaches; potential high-water detour

Points of interest: Dramatic cliff scenery around Pwll Deri; Iron Age forts, including Gawn Fawr; tiny beaches; tranquil coves; pretty Abercastle; Carreg Samson burial chamber; Aber Draw mill ruins

Note: Beyond the hostel at Pwll Deri, there is no accommodation until Trefin, 450 metres from the end of this section; pub and café in Trefin

5: Aber Draw/Trefin to Whitesands Bay

Distance: 11 miles/ 18 kilometres

Terrain: Field paths at start; mildly undulating cliff-top route; surfaced paths and quiet roads at Porthgain and Abereiddy; open heathland on St Davids Head

Points of interest: Industrial heritage at Porthgain, Penclegyr and Abereiddy;

Blue Lagoon at Abereiddy; dramatic cliff scenery; prehistoric remains; good views from St Davids Head; beach at Whitesands Bay

Note: Pub and café in Porthgain, but otherwise few amenities, other than public toilets and seasonal cafés, until St Davids. The tiny city is 3 kilometres off route (bus service) but has a wide range of facilities

6: Whitesands Bay to Solva

Distance: 13 miles/ 21 kilometres

Terrain: Mostly cliff-top paths, but easier going than on previous days; some open heathland, some dunes; occasional surfaced paths and lanes around inlets

Points of interest: City of St Davids, including cathedral and Bishops' Palace; several sites associated with Celtic saints, including St David, St Elvis and St Justinian; views of Ramsey Island; wildflowers; ponies; unusual geology; RNLI lifeboat station at St Justinian's

Note: Accommodation and other facilities in Solva; several campsites en route; good bus links with St Davids means day can be cut short at several points

7: Solva to Broad Haven

Distance: 11 miles/ 18 kilometres

Terrain: Relatively easy cliff-top path, crumbly edges in places; several beaches, including long stretch at Newgale Sands; dunes; some road walking

Points of interest: Attractive harbour village at Solva; well preserved lime

The pretty harbour at Lower Town, Fishguard

kilns; beaches; submerged forest at Newgale Sands; colliery ruins; wildflowers; 'Teletubby House'; landslips

Note: Decent range of facilities in Broad Haven; several B&Bs, campsites and places to eat en route; numerous public toilets

8: Broad Haven to Marloes Sands

Distance: 12½ miles/ 20 kilometres

Terrain: Road walking to start the day; relatively easy cliff-top path; less ascent and descent than on early sections; some quiet lanes

Points on interest: Little Haven; rich flora including woodland of Borough Head; Iron Age forts; 'Waking Eye' sculpture; St Bride's Haven; St Bride's Castle; Mesolithic site on The Nab Head; Marine Nature Reserve and offshore islands; the Deer Park; beach at Marloes Sands

Note: Few facilities beyond Little Haven unless walkers head inland to Marloes village, 1km off route; youth hostel at Marloes Sands, 500 metres from the end of this section

9: Marloes Sands to Sandy Haven

Distance: 13½ miles/ 21 kilometres

Terrain: Cliff-top paths, strenuous in places; some road walking; low-tide crossing of estuary and stony beach (high-tide alternative involves roads, farm tracks and field paths); day ends with cliff-top path

Points of interest: Twentieth-century military remains; fascinating geology, including Cobbler's Hole; lighthouses at St Ann's Head; site of Sea Empress oil tanker disaster; navigational beacons; Henry Tudor's 1485 landing site; Dale village; Pickleridge causeway and lagoons (SSSI); Victorian folly

Dramatic rocks at the ever-popular Marloes Sands

Strategic site: *Pembroke Castle sits on a rocky promontory overlooking the Pembroke River*

Note: Café, pub, shop and B&Bs in Dale; B&Bs and campsite at Sandy Haven, but nowhere to eat

10: Sandy Haven to Pembroke

Distance: 17 miles/ 27 kilometres

Terrain: Low-tide crossing of estuary (high-tide alternative involves roads and field paths); low cliffs; woodland trails and field paths; roads, pavements and promenades through towns

Points of interest: Pretty inlet at Sandy Haven; nineteenth-century Palmerston forts and barracks; LNG jetties and terminals; gardens, statue and Georgian buildings in Milford Haven; Cleddau Bridge; former Royal Navy Dockyard at Pembroke Dock; old harbour buildings beside Pembroke Mill Pond

Note: Plenty of accommodation, shops and other facilities throughout this section

11: Pembroke to Angle

Distance: 11 miles/ 18 kilometres

Terrain: Town roads and paths; woodland trails and field paths; quiet country roads and access lanes across oil company land

Limestone wonder: *The 'Green Bridge of Wales' is a superb natural arch near Castlemartin*

Points of interest: Pembroke Castle; Monkton priory and Old Hall; bluebell woods; Palmerston fort; oil refinery; wildlife in Angle Bay

Note: Good range of facilities in Pembroke and shop in Monkton, but then nothing until Angle where there are two pubs, a limited number of B&Bs, campsite and small shop

12: Angle to St Govan's Chapel

Distance: 17 miles/ 27 kilometres

Terrain: Undulating cliff-top path as far as Freshwater West; sand dunes; quiet roads and roadside trails; field paths; easy walking on limestone cliffs if no live firing on MoD range (alternative uses quiet roads and field paths)

Points of interest: Angle village; Chapel Bay Fort; Thorn Island; beaches at West Angle Bay (SSSI) and Freshwater West; Tudor defences at East Blockhouse; sand dunes; Castlemartin Firing Range; choughs, peregrine falcons and seabird colonies; superb limestone scenery including Green Bridge of Wales and Huntsman's Leap

Note: Beyond Angle, there are few facilities, other than public toilets, until Merrion and on the 'live-firing alternative' route. No shops after Angle

13: St Govan's Chapel to Manorbier

Distance: 11 miles/ 17 kilometres

Terrain: Easy walking on limestone cliffs; more undulating cliff-top section between Stackpole Quay and Manorbier; beaches and dunes

Points of interest: St Govan's Chapel; otters, birds and dragonflies at Bosherston Lily Ponds; Stackpole National Nature Reserve; superb limestone scenery at Stackpole Warren; choughs and seabird colonies, including puffins; beautiful beaches at Broad Haven and Barafundle Bay; Stackpole Quay; Iron Age forts; glow worms at Freshwater East; views across to Devon coast

Note: Café at Stackpole Quay; reasonable facilities in Manorbier including shop

14: Manorbier to Amroth Castle

Distance: 15 miles/ 25 kilometres

Terrain: Cliff-top paths; large expanse of beach/dunes (live-firing alternative involves field path, road walking and surfaced tracks); roads, alleys and paths through towns; woodland trails; surfaced coast path with tunnels along disused railway

Points of interest: Manorbier Castle; King's Quoit burial chamber; fascinating limestone and red sandstone cliff formations; MoD ranges; twentieth-century military remains; large beach/dunes; views of Caldey Island; historic harbour and buildings in Tenby; resort at Saundersfoot; path along disused Saundersfoot Railway, complete with tunnels

Note: Plenty of accommodation, shops and other facilities on this section

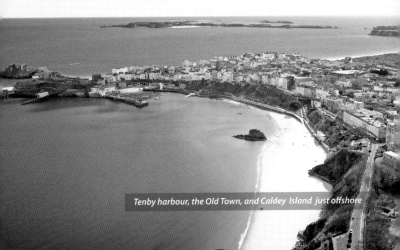

Tenby harbour, the Old Town, and Caldey Island just offshore

Limited for time?
The Pembrokeshire coast in a nutshell

If you have limited time to explore the Pembrokeshire Coast Path — perhaps only a weekend, or even just one day — you might want to consider visiting these unmissable sections.

A superb one-day walk from Stack Rocks to Boshertson via Stackpole Quay provides an opportunity to see some of the most spectacular limestone cliffs in Britain, drop in on St Govan's Chapel and visit the beautiful Bosherston Lily Ponds. With Bosherston as your base and using the Coastal Cruiser bus service, this walk crosses the Castlemartin Firing Range, so you'll need to check whether or not live firing is taking place. The range is usually open to the public at weekends.

Alternatively, for a superb two-day walk along the wilder, more dramatic north coast, make use of the Strumble Shuttle bus to start your walk at Strumble Head and end at Whitesands Bay, near St Davids. With fantastic views to St Davids Head all the while, you'll enjoy some superb cliff scenery, much of it volcanic, as well as a landscape that's dotted with prehistoric remains, including the Carreg Samson cromlech.

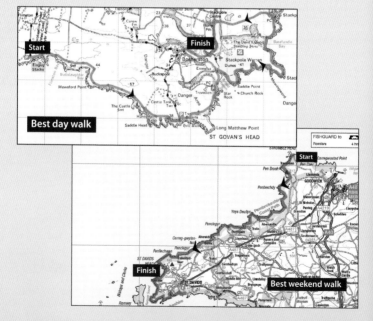

Best day walk
Dramatic limestone cliffs and a National Nature Reserve

Stack Rocks to Bosherston via Stackpole Quay: 9½ miles/ 15 kilometres
Using Bosherston as your base, catch the bus out to Stack Rocks to join the coast path at point 7 on Day Section 12. Heading east, follow the route as far as Stackpole Quay — point 3 on Day Section 13 — and then return to Bosherston via field paths and the Bosherston Lily Ponds.

Bosherston Lily Ponds

Best weekend walk
In prehistoric footsteps on a wild, volcanic coast

Strumble Head to Whitesands Bay: 22½ miles/ 36 kilometres
Day One: 11½ miles/ 18.5 kilometres: Catch the Strumble Shuttle (Fishguard to St Davids) to Strumble Head — Day Section 3, point 4 — then walk the coast path past Pwll Deri, Abercastle and Aber Draw to end the day in Trefin.

Day Two: 11 miles/ 17.5 kilometres: Start of Day Section 5: From Trefin/Aber Draw, walk the coast path to Whitesands Bay, passing through Porthgain and Abereiddy and crossing St Davids Head along the way.

Porthgain harbour

A brief history of the
Pembrokeshire coast

Pembrokeshire boasts a wealth of ancient monuments and other reminders of the distant past

For many thousands of years, humans have had a profound influence on the **Pembrokeshire** coast. Drawn to this far southwestern edge of Wales for a variety of reasons, they have left traces of their lives: anything from Mesolithic rubbish dumps to the forts and ports built by the Victorians. As walkers make their way from St Dogmael's to Amroth Castle, they will come across countless historical sites, each one adding another dimension to the rich experience that comes from walking the Pembrokeshire Coast Path.

The discovery of stone tools near Manorbier and St Bride's Haven as well as middens, or waste heaps, close to cave mouths tell us that Mesolithic

people inhabited the region many thousands of years ago. Leading simple, hunter-gatherer lifestyles, their impact on the landscape was minimal. It was only in the Neolithic period, as people began to settle and farm the land, that they left more enduring traces of their lives... and deaths. Ancient burial sites are scattered throughout the county, including several impressive cromlechs. One of the most famous of these, Carreg Samson, is located just a few hundred metres off the coast path near Abercastle, while others at Manorbier and St Davids Head lie even closer to the route.

Prehistoric forts

Agricultural practices steadily developed during the Bronze Age, but it was really only with the arrival of Celtic tribes, probably from Brittany, between about 500BC and 300BC that more sophisticated farming methods were introduced. The Celts also brought their language, a form of which survives in modern Welsh, as well as more warlike behaviour. With fighting within and between clans a common occurrence, these Iron Age people built promontory forts all along the coast. The ditches and ramparts of many of

Carreg Samson burial chamber overlooks the Wales Coast Path near Abercastle

Hidden gem: *St Govan's chapel is built into a deep cleft in the cliffs*

them can still be clearly seen on dozens of Pembrokeshire headlands. Slightly further inland are the even more impressive remains of Iron Age hill forts including Carn Ingli near Newport and Garn Fawr above Pwll Deri.

Late in the fourth century AD, Celts from Ireland began arriving. The Deisi tribe brought with them the region's first written records: stone tablets containing Latin inscriptions as well as Ogham, an Irish alphabet. Pembrokeshire has the greatest number of Ogham stones found outside of Ireland, including important examples at St Dogmael's and on Caldey Island near Tenby.

The 'Age of Saints'

At about the same time, Irish missionaries began arriving, bringing Christianity to Pembrokeshire. While the Romans had brought their own form of Christianity to many parts of Britain, their armies hadn't bothered much with the far southwest of Wales so this was the region's first significant taste of the new religion. This marks the beginning of the so-called Age of Saints, a period of cultural, linguistic and artistic development in Pembrokeshire and other parts of Wales. Various places in the county have links with these Celtic saints, including St Govan, St Elvis and St Brynach, also known as 'The Irishman'. Not all of these saints came from Ireland; some were homegrown, including the most famous of all, St David, the patron saint of Wales. He was born at St Non's, close to what is now the cathedral city of St Davids. Containing the remains of the saint, the cathedral site became an important place of pilgrimage, with two visits to his shrine being deemed equal to one pilgrimage to Rome.

The Vikings, or, more precisely, Norsemen coming via Ireland, never managed to colonise Wales in the same way as they did eastern England. Raiding parties did, however, attack Pembrokeshire on numerous occasions, plundering St Davids Cathedral at least eight times and killing two of the bishops there. There were a few small Norse settlements established at Milford Haven and Tenby, and some place names reflect this Scandinavian heritage — Skokholm and Skomer, for example.

'Little England beyond Wales'

Following the Battle of Hastings in 1066, the Normans lost no time in marching west and claiming parts of Wales, the southern part of Pembrokeshire being one of the first areas to fall and remain a major stronghold. They brought with them their English supporters and their anglicising influence, leading to this part of the county becoming known as 'Little England beyond Wales'. (For more on the Landsker Line, the line dividing Welsh-speaking Pembrokeshire from English-speaking areas, see page 163.) Norman castles still dot the landscape of southern Pembrokeshire, the most notable being the stronghold at Pembroke — one of the few that never fell to the indigenous Welsh forces.

Over the next few centuries, Pembrokeshire played its part in national events, including Owain Glyndwr's revolt in the early fifteenth century, Henry Tudor's victory over Richard III in the Battle of Bosworth Field in 1485,

The outer curtain walls of Pembroke Castle

Industrial past: *Porthgain harbour once exported slate and crushed roadstone from local quarries*

the English Civil War and various threats of invasion. In all these actions, as throughout the region's history, it was the presence of the sea that created a role for the region. The sea brought raiders, settlers, missionaries and mercenaries. It also brought trade.

Harbours, havens and fishermen

The sometimes tiny harbours and havens that the Pembrokeshire Coast Path drops into and climbs out of every few kilometres or so, have seen goods coming and going by boat for many centuries. The existence of lime kilns in just about every inlet indicates where small vessels once brought limestone in — largely for farmers to use on marginal land — and towns such as Tenby have been home to fishing fleets for a very, very long time. However, it was really only during the Industrial Revolution that some of these places grew to become massive ports, servicing, among other things, the growing trade in coal and the heavy industries that grew up around the mines. The deepwater channel of Milford Haven, home to a naval dockyard as well as the Irish steam packet and a station for US whalers, was deemed so strategically important that a network of sturdy forts was built to protect it from attack by the French. These still stand today. Sadly though, dreams

of large-scale trans-Atlantic trade, boosted by the westward progression of the railways, were never realised and, as in many other areas of Britain, both trade and industry went into fairly rapid decline in the first few decades of the twentieth century. Only Milford Haven saw a significant revival in its international shipping fortunes, becoming a major importer of oil and, more recently, liquefied natural gas.

Industry, farming and tourism

Having struggled with high unemployment for many years, the proportion of Pembrokeshire's population that is out of work is now below the national average. As well as the oil and gas industries, agriculture and tourism play key roles in the area's economy, providing jobs for thousands of people — often overlapping where farms have diversified to provide holiday accommodation or organised activities for visitors. The creation of the Pembrokeshire Coast National Park in 1952 and the Pembrokeshire Coast Path in 1970 represented official recognition of the area's natural beauty and its diverse wildlife — as well as its historical and cultural significance. Along with the opening of the Wales Coast Path in 2012, they will doubtless continue to ensure visitors are able to enjoy this fascinating part of the country for many generations to come.

Wildlife on the Pembrokeshire coast

You're never alone on the Pembrokeshire Coast Path: whether it's seabirds wheeling overhead, seals bobbing up and down in the waters below or ponies grazing the heathland, there's a surprising wealth of animal life along this wonderfully varied section of the Welsh coast. Walk the route in spring or early summer and you'll also be dazzled by the colourful array of wildflowers that adorn the clifftops and grow beside the path. As well as being a National Park, the Pembrokeshire coast has several National Nature Reserves, many Sites of Special Scientific Interest and a Marine Nature Reserve, all helping to protect its diverse habitats.

'Sea pinks' or thrift

Gannets

Guillemots

Small pearl-bordered fritillary

Oystercatchers

A pair of silver-studded blues

Western gorse and heather

Bottlenose dolphins

Atlantic grey seal

Sea campion

Seals, dolphins and choughs

Pembrokeshire's rich and varied habitats are home to a wealth of wildlife

The wide range of habitats along the Pembrokeshire coast gives rise to a huge variety of wildlife — both flora and fauna. From sheer, inaccessible cliffs where vast seabird colonies can nest without fear of predators to mudflats, woods, freshwater ponds, heathland and the open sea itself, all home to countless species of birds, fish, mammals, invertebrates, trees and plants, Pembrokeshire has something to offer the keen naturalist and the casual wildlife observer alike. Keep your eyes peeled as you walk the coast path: there's a lot to see. Although it would be impossible to list all the species you might catch sight of, this chapter provides a guide to some of the most common ones as well as a few of the more elusive characters you may be lucky enough to spot.

Gannets, guillemots and gulls

Birds will undoubtedly become your constant companions as you walk from St Dogmael's to Amroth Castle. Seabirds such as fulmars, kittiwakes, razorbills, common terns, guillemots and a variety of gulls are common sights, particularly during the nesting season when their cliff-face colonies become noisy places that are full of activity. The razorbill, in fact, has been adopted as the symbol of the Pembrokeshire Coast National Park. Cormorants and shags may be spotted in more sheltered waters. Offshore are some of the world's most important colonies of gannets (Grassholm Island) and manx shearwaters (Skomer Island). In a bid to avoid the gulls that prey on them, the latter only leave and return to their burrows under cover of darkness. Puffins and diminutive storm petrels, which spend most of their lives at sea, also breed on the islands. Storm petrels are rarely seen on the mainland, but puffins are occasional visitors to several areas including Stackpole. Having spent the winter at sea, puffin couples usually return to the same burrow each spring, gracing the clifftops from April until August.

A gathering of puffins in breeding plumage on Ramsey Island, off the Pembrokeshire coast

Aerial acrobats: *The Pembrokeshire coast is one of the best places to spot the elusive chough*

Choughs and peregrines

Pembrokeshire is home to almost half of the UK's choughs, but this red-billed, aerobatic member of the crow family remains a rare sight. Your best chances of spotting one are on the Castlemartin cliffs, as well as the islands, particularly in late summer when the young birds are learning flying skills from their parents. Attempts are being made to boost their numbers, partly by allowing ponies to graze the clifftops, thereby reducing the amount of gorse and bracken cover. This, in turn, should help boost numbers of invertebrates, on which choughs feed.

Watch too for peregrine falcons with their distinctive yellow beaks and talons. Nesting on the cliffs, these impressive raptors are just about the fastest creatures on the planet, said to be able to fly at speeds in excess of 100mph when in pursuit of prey.

Other bird species include oystercatchers, lapwings, curlews, ringed plovers and common sandpipers on beaches and mudflats; kestrels, buzzards and ravens; and, on the cliff-top heath and grassland, skylarks, wheatears, yellowhammers and stonechats.

Otters and dolphins

As far as mammals go, you may occasionally spot stoats, badgers, weasels and roe deer, particularly early or late in the day. Otters are making a come-back in many parts of Britain and are often seen at dawn and dusk in the Bosherston Lily Ponds and in the Milford Haven waterway. You'll need to be both quiet and patient if you hope to catch a glimpse of one though. Otter-spotters often have to console themselves with other signs of these beautiful mammals, including their droppings — or spraints. Solitary male otters and family groups have their own territories, which they mark by leaving smelly spraints in prominent locations such as on large boulders or at the base of tree trunks. The droppings tend to be black and tarry, with a lot of fish bones in them. But the only sure-fire way of recognising an otter spraint is to sniff it; its smell has been variously described as fishy or like freshly-mown hay, jasmine tea or lavender.

For a better chance of spotting mammals, turn your binoculars towards the sea. The nutrient-rich waters brought by the Gulf Stream allow a range of creatures to thrive in the seas off Pembrokeshire, including seals, porpoises and dolphins. Strumble Head is a particularly good place for spotting cetaceans, and sightings here include large number of harbour porpoises and common dolphins as well as occasional reports of Risso's and bottle-nosed dolphins and, further out to sea, basking sharks, minke whales and even orca.

At low tide, grey seals often haul out on the rocks around Strumble Head, although they can be seen in many other parts of Pembrokeshire too. Ramsey Island, for example, is home to southern Britain's largest colony of grey seals. From August through to the late autumn, females begin arriving on sheltered beaches and in some larger sea caves to give birth to their pups, which are covered in soft white fur for the first few weeks of their lives. December to February is a good time to spot seals. This is when large numbers of adults congregate on beaches to moult.

Marine Nature Reserves

The ecological importance of the seas off Pembrokeshire is recognised by the fact that the county is home to one of the UK's four Marine Nature Reserves (MNR) — around Skomer Island and the Marloes peninsula. These reserves have a similar status and level of protection to National Nature Reserves, but were set up specifically to protect marine habitats and wildlife as well as other features on the seabed and along the shore. This means fishing activities are strictly controlled and a speed limit is enforced. The Skomer MNR, which covers more than 1,300 hectares (3,200 acres), was established in 1990. The area's conservation priorities include grey seals, some species of seaslugs, a horny coral known as pink seafan, eelgrass, sea urchins, crawfish as well as algal and sponge communities.

Maritime wildflowers

Pembrokeshire is renowned for its spectacularly colourful wildflower displays during the spring and early summer. Late May and June are probably the best times to enjoy this beautiful spectacle. The most common, and easily identifiable species are bluebells, ox-eye daisies, thrift and sea campion, but watch too for the yellow burst associated with tormentil, birdsfoot trefoil and cowslip. Easier to miss are the dainty flowers of herb Robert and spring squill.

Widespread across the heath and scrubland are gorse, a thorny plant whose yellow flowers can be seen at almost any time of the year; heather, which carpets the slopes in purple blooms in the late summer; and bracken, a prolific fern that quickly overwhelms most other species where it takes hold. Blackthorn and bramble also figure highly on the clifftops — and would probably overwhelm the coast path in places if it wasn't for the work of the wardens who carry out a systematic programme of cutting and trimming throughout the summer months.

Lichen and thrift, or 'sea pinks', colour the rocks

Keep still: *A timid common lizard emerges from the pathside heather*

Lizards and butterflies

The heathland vegetation hides a number of reptiles, including common lizards, slow worms, grass snakes and adders. Don't be alarmed if you stumble across any of these: the only one that can hurt you is the adder, Britain's only venomous snake, and these will usually make themselves scarce as soon as they sense your approach. They bite only as a last resort: if you tread on one or try to pick one up. Even then, the worst symptoms of an adder bite are likely to be nausea and severe bruising.

The wide range of vegetation along the Pembrokeshire coast inevitably gives rise to a wide range of butterflies. Thirty species have been recorded on the Stackpole estate alone, including the silver-studded blue butterfly, which is almost extinct in most of the rest of the UK apart from Dorset and Hampshire. Much more common are the peacock, small tortoiseshell, orange-tip, dark green fritillary, brown argus, ringlet, common blue and the well camouflaged grayling.

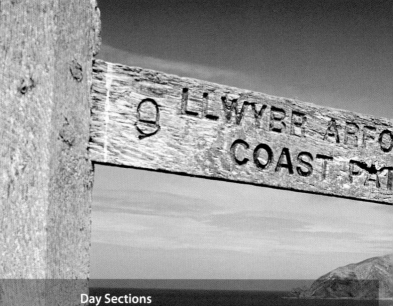

Day Sections

Llwybr Arfordir Cymru
Wales Coast Path

The Pembrokeshire
section of the
Wales Coast Path

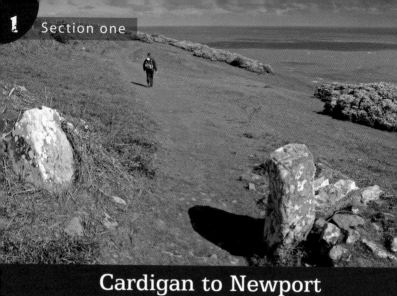

Cardigan to Newport

Distance: *27 kilometres / 17 miles* | **Start:** *Cardigan SN 177 458*
Finish: *Newport (Iron Bridge over the Nevern River) SN 062 394* | **Maps:** *OS Explorer OL35 North Pembrokeshire, Landranger 145 Cardigan & Mynydd Preseli*

Outline: A long, tough day along the top of wild, rugged and relatively remote cliffs, always surrounded by dramatic coastal scenery.

The first day is one of the toughest — it's long, there's a lot of ascent and descent and there are no facilities en route. Having said that, this section contains some of the wildest and most rugged coastal scenery of the entire route. Dramatic cliffs, stacks, arches, caves and other impressive geological features are the order of the day. In spring and early summer, wildflowers grace the clifftops. A gentle descent to the Nevern estuary and the beautifully situated town of Newport makes for a fine way to end a superb first day.

Services: *Cardigan has a good range of facilities, including accommodation, places to eat, cash machines and shops. (Cardigan TIC at Theatr Mwldan | 01239 613230.) St Dogmael's has a range of accommodation, a shop and places to eat. There's a campsite, youth hostel and seasonal café at Poppit Sands.* **Please note***: the is no drinking water available on this section. There's another seasonal café with nearby public toilets at Newport Sands. Newport has accommodation, places to eat, shops, a chemist, a bank with cash machine, launderette and public toilets. Robins Taxi, Cardigan | 01239 612190*

👁 **Don't miss:** St Dogmael's – picturesque twelfth-century abbey ruins just off route | **Witches' Cauldron** – collapsed sea cave beside coast path | **Nevern River estuary** – rich and varied birdlife

▲ *Striding along the cliffs at the start of the Pembrokeshire section of the Wales Coast Path*

Cardigan/Aberteifi

The colourful market town of Cardigan, or Aberteifi, sits close to the mouth of River Teifi — at the point where the counties of Pembrokeshire and Ceredigion meet. A walled town first developed around the Norman castle — built at the end of the eleventh century by Roger de Montgomery — and for the next 200 years or so, control of the stronghold and its settlement changed hands several times.

Sea trade formed an important role in the growth of Cardigan through the centuries. In the town's early days, woollen cloth was exported to France, while corn and limestone were among the products being imported. By the early part of the eighteenth century, a substantial herring trade had developed alongside the import and export of products as diverse as ale, salt, prunes and oranges. The main industries were shipbuilding and brick-making.

Visitors to modern-day Cardigan will find a friendly, compact town where Welsh is widely spoken. The castle is a community and educational facility open to the public. Other interesting buildings in the town include the Guildhall and adjoining Market Hall. Commissioned in 1856, these were the first civic buildings in Britain to be designed in the 'modern Gothic' style.

The old bridge in the centre of Cardigan

The route: **Cardigan to Newport**

1 This section of the Wales Coast Path begins by the bronze **Otter Statue** on **Prince Charles Quay**, below **Cardigan Castle** — on the north side of the **Teifi Bridge**.

Cross the bridge and turn right onto the **B4546** 'St Dogmaels' road. Within 50 metres, turn left up a track. Around 300 metres later, turn right and follow the waymarks as the Wales Coast Path zigzags across field edges, to cross the **Ceredigion/Pembrokeshire border** at a bridge over a small stream.

When the path enters **St Dogmael's**, turn right into **David Street** and immediately left into **Shingrig**, passing the ruins of the 12th-century, Benedictine 👁 **St Dogmael's Abbey** on your left.

Beyond the Abbey, turn left and, when you reach the **High Street**, go left again. Roughly 50 metres later, look out for an **alleyway** on the right. The waymarked path soon skirts a playing field and passes the **Teifi Netpool Inn**, before following the path on the west bank of **Afon Teifi** to come out onto the road to 'Poppit Sands'.

Turn right, past the **Ferry Inn**, and you will shortly arrive at the marker for the **official start of the Pembrokeshire Coast Path National Trail**.

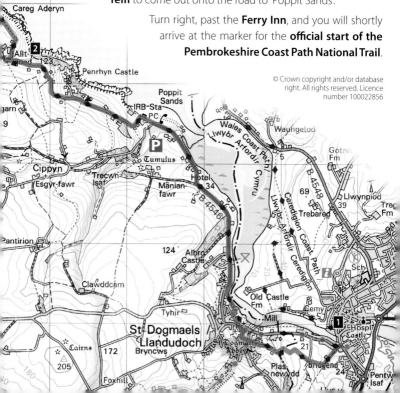

Walking north along the road and keeping the river on your right, head out of the village. After passing the **Webley Hotel** on the left, you have uninterrupted views of the estuary and its mudbanks.

About 2.5 kilometres after leaving St Dogmael's, you will pass the RNLI's **Poppit Sands lifeboat station** on your right. To the left is a seasonal beach café. The road, narrower now, swings left here and soon begins climbing. Follow this pleasant lane past the **youth hostel** and out to the **Allt y Coed Farm** campsite.

2 After crossing the cattle grid at the lane-end, keep right on the gently descending track. Bear right at the next fork, dropping past the campsite. The track passes in front of the farm buildings to reach a pair of gates. Go through the small gate on the right. After the next gate, you are on an enclosed path. Nearing the end of this path, go through another small gate on the right.

The route now crosses open ground that is covered in bluebells and the yellow flowers of gorse in the spring. Soon after the path rounds **Cemaes Head**, it passes through two gates in quick succession. After the next stile, it passes to the right of an abandoned coastguard lookout post before continuing along a more exposed section of clifftop.

Saltmarsh at the southern end of Poppit Sands

Rugged coast: *Looking back along the cliffs towards Pen yr Afr*

Grassy slopes drop away to the right, coming to an abrupt end at the dark rock slabs just above the crashing waves. In the distance, Dinas Island and Strumble Head can be seen, visited later on the trail. At 175 metres above sea level, the highest point on the entire Pembrokeshire Coast Path is passed close to Pen yr Afr.

A sign beside the next stile warns of the perils of the clifftop path to Newport Sands: not only does it entail an awful lot of ups and downs, it is exposed to the elements and doesn't pass through any settlements of significant size. The only village between here and the car park at Newport Sands is Moylgrove — and even that's more than 1 kilometre off route (*See detour, below*).

3 About 2.5 kilometres after rounding Cemaes Head, the path drops almost to sea level to cross **Pwllygranant**. At a fingerpost, ignore the path up to the left; instead, drop to cross the stream via a wooden bridge and then climb steeply back on to the cliffs. The first of several descents almost to sea level.

The remarkable geology along this section of the coast will undoubtedly slow your progress as you gaze down on impossibly steep slopes and extraordinary folds in the rock (see pages 80-81 for geology notes). The cliffs consist of alternating layers of sandstone and mudstone, produced around 440 million years ago and then compressed and forced upwards by the collision of continents some 50 million years later during the period known to geologists as the 'Caledonian Orogeny'.

4 Coming in from the cliffs slightly, cross a track leading to a long, white cottage and then turn right after the gate on the other side. Descending gently, make sure you swing right soon after the next gate. There is a bench on the left at this bend — a good place to sit and watch the waves crashing on the rocks below.

Cross the stone bridge over the stream entering **Ceibwr Bay** and then swing left along the track. Look to the right here and you'll see the first of many lime kilns encountered along the coast path. This one is very small and partly covered by vegetation; there are many better examples further along the route, including one beside the Nevern River on the edge of Newport.

Turn right on reaching a lane and then right again at the next junction.

Detour: *To Moylgrove village*

Turn left along the lane for around 1 kilometre to reach **Moylgrove**. This pretty village has two B&Bs and a licensed café serving lunches and teas.

Continuing on the **official route**, immediately after passing a bench, take the path on the

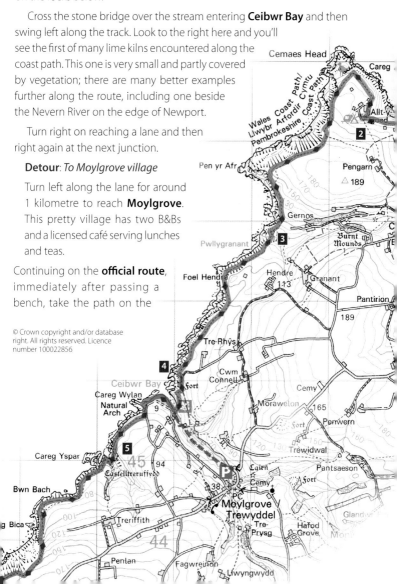

Room to breathe: *Heading for Newport with the hills of Carningli Common in the background*

right, to pass through a tunnel of vegetation that leads out on to the low cliff along the southern side of Ceibwr Bay. After crossing a grassy area, climb back to the road, along which you turn right. After about 100 metres of road walking, you reach a fingerpost: turn right here to regain the clifftop path. Caves, stacks and natural arches are common features along this next section of the coast.

5 After dropping down a few steps, the route passes to the right of one of Pembrokeshire's most impressive geological features: **Pwll y Wrach** or the 👁 **Witches' Cauldron**. This enormous chasm was created by the collapse of the roof of a sea cave. The path crosses a land bridge over the mouth of the cauldron, below which a narrow passage connects the hole to the sea. It is best seen in retrospect — after crossing a wooden bridge and then climbing the other side of the valley.

The route now passes **Carreg Yspar**, a large, grass-topped lump of rock that, at first sight, appears to be an island. Closer inspection of the cliffs to the right reveals that it is, in fact, joined to the mainland by a precipitous neck of rock.

In May and June, these cliffs are a riot of colour: as well as bluebells, the yellow of the gorse and the pink sea thrift, watch for the star-like, blue-lilac flowers of spring squill, the delicate pink spires of the common spotted orchid and sea campion's white trumpets.

After miles of exposed walking, you finally descend from the high cliffs and can see Newport — day's end — ahead. The route drops to cross a bridge over a small stream and then climbs on to low cliffs above Newport Sands.

Lime kilns

Almost every inlet on the Milford Haven waterway has a lime kiln or two. Most are fairly small, set up by individual farmers to fertilise the land. Small sailing ships would unload their cargo of local limestone and this would have been burned with coal and clay to produce lime for the fields, counteracting excessive soil acidity. The practice dates back to the Middle Ages and continued well into the nineteenth century.

The atmospheric hills of Carningli Common, dotted with Bronze Age settlements, burial cairns and an Iron Age fort, form a handsome backdrop to these last few kilometres. The Celtic saint, Brynach, is said to have conversed with divine messengers while seeking refuge in a cave on these rocky uplands. The name Carningli could be a corruption of the Welsh for 'Mountain of the Angels'.

These hills are almost undoubtedly the source of the bluestones that make up much of the inner circle of Stonehenge: the spotted dolerite rock from which they are formed is found in only one place in the UK — other than as erratics — and that's west Wales. The tors at Carn Clust-y-ci and Carn Llwyd are thought to be likely contenders, although other sources slightly

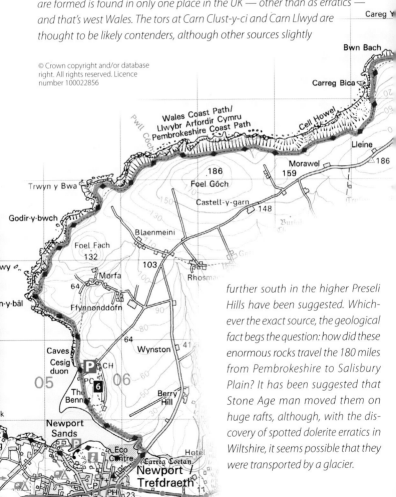

further south in the higher Preseli Hills have been suggested. Whichever the exact source, the geological fact begs the question: how did these enormous rocks travel the 180 miles from Pembrokeshire to Salisbury Plain? It has been suggested that Stone Age man moved them on huge rafts, although, with the discovery of spotted dolerite erratics in Wiltshire, it seems possible that they were transported by a glacier.

Day's end: *The final section of path before the town of Newport*

6 Descending to the car park at **Newport Sands**, cross the lane and then pass to the left of the toilet block to enter and cross the southern half of the car park. Exit via a small wooden gate. Waymarker posts now guide you across a golf course.

Entering a shrubby area, keep left at a fork close to a waymarker post, but then ignore another path to the left near a building. The path passes a limekiln beside the 👁 **Nevern estuary** or **Afon Nyfer**.

The estuary here is home to a rich variety of birdlife, including widgeon, goldeneye, Brent geese, goosander, kingfisher, heron, little egret and a variety of gulls. At low tide, watch for waders such as redshank, curlew and oystercatcher searching for a tasty meal in the exposed mudflats.

On reaching the road, turn right to cross the 1894-built **Iron Bridge** over the Nevern River. The first section of the route ends here. The next section begins by going through the small gate on the right after the bridge, but the village of **Newport** can be reached by continuing up the road and then turning right at the T-junction.

Newport to Fishguard

Distance: *18 kilometres / 11 miles* | **Start:** *Newport (Iron Bridge over the Nevern River) SN 062 394* | **Finish:** *Fishguard (Lower Town) SM 962 371* | **Maps:** *Ordnance Survey Explorer OL35 North Pembrokeshire, Landrangers 145 Cardigan & Mynydd Preseli and 157 St David's & Haverfordwest*

Outline: Another wonderful day following a roller-coaster clifftop route dipping in and out of small coves backed by surprisingly verdant valleys. The cliffs on this section may not be as high as on the previous day, but they are just as wild and rugged. One of the highlights is Dinas Island, which isn't an island at all but a wedge of land divided from the 'mainland' by a glacial meltwater channel. The path climbs its steep slopes to reach Dinas Head – at 142 metres, the highest point on this section. Fishguard is entered via the pretty harbour, once busy with trading vessels but now home to leisure boats.

Services: *Newport has accommodation, places to eat, shops, a chemist, a bank with cash machine, launderette and public toilets. (Newport TIC: 01239 820912; new-portTIC@pembrokeshirecoast.org.uk.) Toilets at Parrog and Cwm-Yr-Eglwys. Pub and toilets at Pwllgwaelod near Dinas Island. Campsites on Dinas Island and at Penrhyn. The latter has a seasonal shop that is open to non-campers. The town of Fishguard has a good range of facilities, including accommodation, places to eat, cash machines, shops and a launderette. Carrots Cabs, Fishguard | 01348 872088*

Don't miss: Cwm-yr-Eglwys – St Brynach's, a twelfth-century, Celtic-style church | **Fishguard Fort** – ruins with cannons pointing out to sea | **Fishguard Lower Town** – pretty, harbourside settlement

▲ *High cliffs west of Dinas Head*

Newport

Newport grew up around the Norman castle built here by the Fitzwilliam family in the twelfth century. It follows a typical Norman 'new town' layout with its streets running north-south in a grid pattern. The castle fell into disrepair in the sixteenth century, but was then renovated about 300 years later. Today, it is a private home.

There is plenty of evidence of prehistoric dwellers in the area from Mesolithic times onwards, but it was only after the Normans established their town that it began to prosper — largely as a result of the medieval wool trade. By the sixteenth century, the area known as Parrog had become a busy centre for maritime trade and shipbuilding. Ships came into the port laden with lime and coal, and would leave with herrings, slate, wool and cloth. Over the years, the river silted up and it is now too shallow to cope with anything but small fishing vessels and leisure boats: the last ocean-bound trader left these waters in 1934. However, the maritime links continue and one of the many warehouses built at Parrog is now home to a boat club.

Newport today is a friendly, attractive town with some great places to eat and wide-ranging facilities for walkers on the coast path.

Looking back across Newport Sands

The route: **Newport to Fishguard**

1 Starting from the southern side of the **Iron Bridge** over the **Nevern River,** go through the small gate to access a constructed path that leads through woodland beside the estuary. Several tracks and paths lead up to the left — into the main part of **Newport** — but coastal walkers should follow the path until it comes out on to a road at **Parrog**. Turn right here. You'll quickly pass a phone box, public toilets and car park on the right. *The latter has an old lime kiln and the remains of a lime burners' hut in it.*

2 Follow the lane round to the left, passing in front of the **Morawelon Café**. Take the path to the right of the entrance to the campsite. Running alongside the harbour wall, this passes some lovely old cottages and comes out opposite the gate to **Rock House**. You now have a choice depending on the state of the tide. For two hours either side of high tide, you will have to use the high-tide alternative.

> **Alternative high-tide route**: *Inland route avoiding the shore*
> Turn left and follow the lane uphill for about 600 metres. At a crossing of lanes, turn right. When the track forks, look to your right and you will see a large metal gate. Just to the right of this, hidden by the bushes, is a stile. Cross this and walk with the field boundary on your left. After the stile in the bottom of the field, turn right along the track. Keep left at the fork and then join a footpath to the right of **Maes Y Brenin**'s gate. Then turn left when you reach the coast path.

At low tide, turn right at **Rock House** and then left along the beach. After about 50 metres, go up the slipway. Bear right up a surfaced lane in front of some cottages. This narrows to become a path that crosses a **small stream**.

Broad sands: *Newport north beach seen from the Parrog*

The high-tide and low-tide routes now meet up again and the **official route** soon makes its way out on to the cliffs.

Just before you drop back to sea level, look down to the right and, at low tide, you'll see a good example of a wave-cut platform. These flat areas of rock at the base of the cliffs are created by the sea steadily undermining the cliff, eventually causing it to collapse. The rubble from the collapse then forms a level platform.

Repeated over time, the process can sometimes result in platforms stretching some distance from the base of the cliffs.

Drop to sea level to cross a bridge where **Cwm Rhigian** reaches the sea — this is the first of today's many descents to sea level. Cross a pebbly ridge at the back of the bay: a storm beach thrown up by particularly fierce waves. The path then climbs back on to the cliffs again.

Watch for a narrow, steep-sided cleft, or zawn, in the cliffs in a few hundred metres. Created by differential erosion of the rocks, there are many examples of these along the Pembrokeshire coast, some of the finest being found in the Stackpole and Manorbier areas.

The cliffs in this area are prone to erosion, and landslips are not uncommon. In a few places, the coast path has tumbled away into the sea and the National Trail has had to be moved a few metres back from the edge. The cliffs receive a battering from the sea, particularly during storms; a process that constantly undermines them — as seen in the formation of wave-cut platforms. But it is heavy rain that often does the most noticeable damage to the cliff-tops, causing saturated ground to become unstable and simply 'slip' away in sudden and dramatic fashion.

3 A flight of steps leads down to **Aber Fforest**, an idyllic cove that is home to a particularly well preserved **lime kiln**. On reaching a rough track, turn right and then cross the bridge at the back of the bay. As you climb the other side of the valley, bear right at a fork.

4 Eventually, you reach a surfaced lane. Turn right to drop into 👁 **Cwm-yr-Eglwys**, one of Pembrokeshire's most popular beauty spots. Nestling close to the eastern edge of **Dinas Island**, it is a peaceful spot, sheltered from the prevailing south-westerly winds. Turn right at the bottom of the slope and then swing left to pass the **ruined church** on your right.

This is St Brynach's, a twelfth-century, Celtic-style church. Once large enough to hold a congregation of 300, all that remains today are the belfry and part of the west wall. Some of the building and its accompanying churchyard were lost during a big storm in 1979, but much of the original damage to the site occurred 120 years earlier. It was in October 1859 that a massive storm hit the area, thought to be one of the biggest tempests experienced in the Irish Sea during the whole of the nineteenth century. With wind speeds of more than 160km/h, it wrecked 114 ships along the Welsh coast including, famously, the Royal Charter, which was smashed to pieces on the Anglesey coast, resulting in the deaths of 450 people.

The pretty hamlet of Cwm-yr-Eglwys, tucked below Dinas Head

Storm damage: *The remains of St Brynach's, the twelfth-century church at Cwm-yr-Eglwys*

The storm resulted in the development, in 1860, of the Meteorological Office's first gale warning service.

At the church gate is a model of a coastal trading brig, the type of boat that suffered the most losses during the 1859 storm. They were of shallow draft and relatively flat bottomed, allowing them to be sailed into bays at high water and then unloaded at low tide by horse and cart.

5 From the **toilet block** in Cwm-yr-Eglwys, follow the lane round to the right. (For a short-cut that leaves out the superb circuit of **Dinas Island**, see the 'alternative route' below. It'd be a shame to miss out on the so-called island, especially considering the short-cut only reduces section two by about 2.7 kilometres. Walkers are probably more likely to be swayed by the difference in height gain — the 'island' circuit involving an extra 250 metres of ascent.)

After climbing briefly, you reach a pair of gates with a no-entry sign on it. Cross the **footbridge** on the right here. The path eventually emerges from the trees and the sumptuous vegetation on this sheltered side of Dinas Island, allowing you to enjoy the glory of the clifftops again. Bear right at a waymarked fork.

Needle Rock, *just below the next set of steps, is crowded with noisy nesting guillemots and razorbills in the summer. Like their auk relative, the puffin, both*

All you survey: *Gazing out over the Irish Sea from Dinas Head*

species look rather clumsy on land, but their short wings make them excellent swimmers. They spend most of the year at sea, coming to land only at nesting time. Their numbers, packed on to tiny ledges on Needle Rock, are quite impressive.

Keep right at any forks and you will eventually reach the 'trig' pillar on **Pen y Fan** — at 142 metres, the highest point on **Dinas Head** and an excitingly exposed place on a windy day. Up until now, the 'island' path has wound its way around the cliff face, but, from here, as it heads south-west, it keeps to the top of the high ground. Having rounded Dinas Head, you now have an uninterrupted view into Fishguard Bay and across to Goodwick's unusually long North Breakwater. Where the path begins descending more steeply, bear left at a fork, keeping back from the crumbly cliff edge.

Turn right along a surfaced track and drop to the tiny beach, pub and public toilets at **Pwllgwaelod**.

The **Old Sailors pub** *and restaurant is said to date back to the late sixteenth century. It was originally called the* Sailor's Safety, *because of the light it burned at nights as a guide to ships. In more recent times, it was one of the writer Dylan Thomas's favourite watering-holes.*

Thomas, born in Swansea in 1914, is probably best known for his poetry and for his play Under Milk Wood. Originally written for radio, it was first performed in 1954, starring the famous Welsh actor Richard Burton. In 1972, a big-screen adaptation of the play was filmed in Fishguard's Old Town, where today's section of the walk ends. This also starred Richard Burton, this time joined by Elizabeth Taylor and Peter O'Toole.

JuliusKielaitis / Shutterstock.com

Fishguard's ferries

Walkers will often see ferries shuttling between Fishguard and Rosslare in Ireland. Cunard's trans-Atlantic liners used to call in here too. To build the port, almost two million tonnes of rock had to be blasted from the cliffs. Much of this was used to construct the 610-metre long North Breakwater. Ironically, it was the East Breakwater, built in 1913, that stopped this trade, causing the harbour to silt up and so preventing larger liners from docking.

Dramatic seacliffs: *The view ahead from Dinas Head*

Alternative route: *To cut the corner across the neck of Dinas Island*

Turn left along the fenced path immediately in front of the toilets — a fingerpost indicates this is a wheelchair-accessible path to 'Pwllgwaelod'. It crosses a car park and enters a small caravan site via a gate. A clear path leads across the grass and then you join a surfaced path that heads out along the edge of the wetlands. *This alternative route may not be as beautiful or as exciting as the walk around Dinas Head, but it is rich in terms of wildlife and geological interest. The valley,* **Cwm Dewi**, *is a meltwater channel, eroded when an ice sheet covering north Pembrokeshire during the last glacial period began to melt. Watch out for the increasingly rare pearl-bordered fritillary butterfly, adders, frogs and birds such as willow warblers and blackcaps.* Turn left along the lane at **Pwllgwaelod** to rejoin the main route.

6 On the **official route**, as soon as the lane begins climbing, turn right to rejoin the cliff path. A stile at the top of the steps leads into a field. Keep close to the fence and hedgerow on your right, and another stile soon leads back on to the clifftop path. You may not be aware of the cliff edge at first because of the dense thickets of gorse and hawthorn on your right. These are a common feature as far as Fishguard now, unfortunately blocking the seaward view at times, but also, thankfully, providing shelter from the wind on wild days.

After the next stile, the grazing land comes right to the cliff edge. Cross this area and then go round to the left of a short section of old wall. You now have a fence on your left, but only for a short while. At the fence corner, turn right. A series of yellow arrows indicates the route on this small headland.

Drop to cross a bridge above the grey beach of **Pwll Gwylog**. The path then continues, crossing a series of stiles: sometimes on the seaward side of the fence, sometimes on the landward side. *Inland, the tors of Pembrokeshire's northern hills are clearly visible, adding a wild beauty to an already rugged scene.*

The path gradually drops to **Aber Bach**, the mouth of which contains some of the most impressive stacks seen so far on the walk. *These rock fangs, particularly those to the west of the cove, provide some shelter from the prevailing winds, making the beach here a good place to enjoy a paddle. What better on a hot day than the chance to revive your feet in the cool sea?!* At the fingerpost at the back of the bay, ignore the path up to the left; simply keep straight on, across grass and pebbles, to cross the **bridge**.

Beyond the gate at the top, turn right along the lane. After about 150 metres of road walking, climb the steps on the right — beside a fingerpost. The sheltered path soon leads back out on to the cliff.

7 A gate leads into '**Fishguard Bay Caravan and Camping Park**'. Walk across the grassy area and then turn right along the main track through the site. There's a small **shop**, which welcomes walkers and sells basic provisions, set back on the right here. Take the next track on the left and, as this swings left, cross the grass, making for a gate between two static caravans. As you head back on to the cliffs, you get

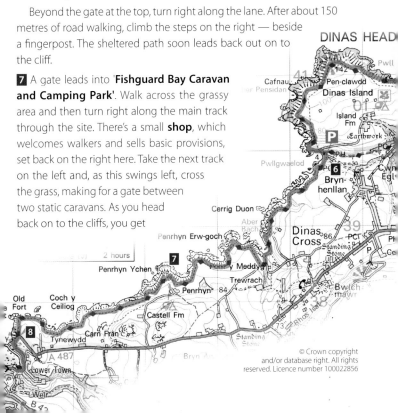

The 'Green Bridge of Wales', near Castlemartin in south Pembrokeshire

Coastal geology

Millions of years of history laid bare for all to see

Nothing brings geology and geomorphology to life quite like a coastal walk. Here, in the folds of the exposed rock strata and in the stacks, arches and wave-cut platforms, earth processes are clear for all to see. And the Pembrokeshire Coast Path has more to offer than most — in fact, the area's outstanding geology was one of the reasons why the Pembrokeshire Coast National Park was established.

In general terms, the oldest rocks, some as much as 600 million years old, are found in north Pembrokeshire, while south Pembrokeshire has the 'youngest', although none of these is less than about 280 million years old.

The most common rocks along the north coast — slates, shales, sandstones and mudstones — are sedimentary rocks dating from the

Fossilised seabed ripples near Amroth

Ordovician period, about 485 to 440 million years ago. Further south, the shales and limestone that form the Marloes Pennisula and Skomer Island, were laid down in the Silurian period, about 440 to 420 million years ago.

Younger still are the old red sandstones, a visually striking form of sedimentary rock found in south Pembrokeshire. This was created during the Devonian period, about 420 to 359 years ago. But some of the youngest rocks are those associated with the Carboniferous period, including the limestone around Castlemartin and Lydstep — formed between about 360 and 325 million years ago — and, further east, around Saundersfoot and Amroth Castle, coal measures that are a mere 300 million years old.

All these rocks have been subject to a variety of earth processes during their long lifetimes: the uplift associated with mountain-building events, marine erosion, weathering, glaciation. The latter resulted from the climate being considerably colder between two million and 12,000 years ago. Sometimes the ice sheet covering Pembrokeshire was huge, stretching as far south as Devon; sometimes, only the

Tilted strata in a cave at Newgale

> ## "Geology is the music of the earth"
>
> Hans Cloos, *twentieth-century German geologist*

northern part of the county would have been covered. The last glacial period ended roughly 12,000 years ago, resulting in the creation of drowned valleys or rias along the Pembrokeshire coast, including Milford Haven.

But earth processes didn't end with the melting of the last ice-sheet; they continue today. Most are imperceptible, creeping along at a snail's pace, slowly creating features such as wave-cut platforms and sand dunes. But, just occasionally, they make their presence felt and a landslip, rock fall or other coastal drama will be witnessed.

More information: For more details, visit the geology pages on the Pembrokeshire Coast National Park website: www.pembrokeshire-coast.org.uk

Harbour guardian: *Eighteenth-century Fishguard Fort still sports several iron cannon*

a great view of the second **Needle Rock** of the day. *It's not hard to see how this one got its name: the base of the narrow stack is pierced by an arch, just like the 'eye' of a needle.*

The next gate leads on to National Trust land at **Castell**. Ignore the path to the left at the next fingerpost; simply continue beside the fence and then an old wall on the left. There are a few more relatively gentle ups and downs before you reach the remains of 👁 **Fishguard Fort** on **Castle Point.**

The fort was built in 1781 as a direct response to a raid on Fishguard by an American privateer a couple of years earlier. During the skirmish, one of the town's ships was captured and a ransom demanded. Having paid off the privateer, the townsfolk decided it was about time they built themselves a fort. It was originally armed with eight nine-pounder guns. The fort played a minor role in the French 'invasion' of 1797 (see section three for more details), but it fell into disrepair after the end of the Napoleonic wars in 1815. As well as the stone gateway and some walls, modern visitors to the site will see four cannons pointing out to sea and a small building with an intact barrel roof.

8 To explore the ruins, go through the stone gateway on your right immediately after a gate beside the fort; the main route, however, goes left. Turn right just before reaching a small car park. The path comes out on to a road, along which you turn right. On rounding the bend, you are able to look down into the old part of 🐚 **Fishguard**, known as **Lower Town** (Cwm).

The pretty harbourside buildings of Lower Town mostly date back to the eighteenth century, when Fishguard was busy with trading vessels, a herring fishery and some shipbuilding. At one point, it is said to have had 50 ships, trading largely with Bristol, Ireland and Liverpool. The most common imports were coal, food, cloth and limestone with ships leaving laden with oats, barley, herrings and wool. The harbour was built around the drowned northern end of Cwm Gwaun, another meltwater channel like Dinas Island's Cwm Dewi. Today, like so many of the older ports visited on the Pembrokeshire Coast Path, it is used only by small craft, mostly leisure boats. One of the old warehouses still stands proud in the car park on the western side of the quay; on the opposite side of the water, the Fishguard Bay Yacht Club occupies an old flour store. If time allows, it's worth having a wander round this charming old waterside location and the quaint cottages that cling to the hillside above it.

As well as being used as Llareggub, the fictional Welsh fishing village in the 1972 film version of Under Milk Wood, Lower Town was also used as a setting in the 1955 film Moby Dick, starring Gregory Peck.

As you reach the first of the cottages, watch for a dead-end turning on the left. Immediately turn right along an alley, almost back on yourself. This turning is easy to miss, so watch carefully for it.

On reaching a road, cross straight over and make for the river. Turn left along the riverside path and then exit the car park to the left of an **old bridge.** Turn right along the road. The main part of **Fishguard** can now be reached by continuing straight up the road, but the official coast path — and section three of our route — continues through the car park on the right immediately after the road bridge.

Boats moored in the harbour at Lower Town, Fishguard

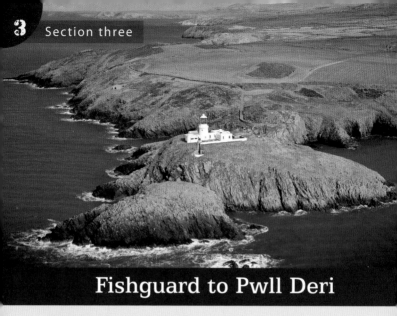

Fishguard to Pwll Deri

Distance: *17 kilometres / 10½ miles* | **Start:** *Fishguard (Lower Town) SM 962 371*
Finish: *Pwll Deri Youth Hostel SM 892 387* | **Maps:** *Ordnance Survey Explorer OL35 North Pembrokeshire, Landranger 157 St David's & Haverfordwest*

Outline: A varied day, starting on town paths, crossing heathland and ending with spectacular cliffs and a good chance of spotting wildlife.

After skirting the edge of Fishguard, the coastal path heads back on to the cliffs, the sense of remoteness growing with every step. Much of the clifftop is heathland, rich in birdlife; seals, porpoises and even dolphins can be spotted around dramatic Strumble Head. The final few kilometres are completed in the spectacular surroundings of Pwll Deri and its mighty cliffs. Walkers will need to stock up before leaving Goodwick: there are no cafés or pubs until Trefin at the end of section four and no shops until St Davids at the end of section five.

Services: *Between them, the adjoining settlements of Fishguard and Goodwick have a range of facilities, including accommodation, places to eat, cash machines, shops and launderette. (Fishguard TIC| 01437 776636; fishguard.tic@pembrokeshire.gov.uk.) The last public toilets of the day are in Goodwick. There's a B&B 10 minutes off route in Llanwnda and a campsite off route in Tresinwen. Otherwise, no accommodation until the youth hostel at Pwll Deri. Carrots Cabs, Fishguard: 01348 872088*

Don't miss: Art on The Parrog – murals and mosaics depicting local history | **Carreg Goffa memorial** – marks the last landing of foreign forces on British soil | **Strumble Head** – dramatically positioned lighthouse

▲ *Strumble Head lighthouse*

Fishguard

Fishguard is divided into three distinct and very different areas: the old harbour of Lower Town; the modern town of Fishguard; and Goodwick, originally a fishing village but enlarged at the beginning of the twentieth century to house port and railway workers. Goodwick and the main part of Fishguard are separated by a long stretch of sand and shingle beach. If it's facilities you're looking for, the modern town has the widest choice, but if charm is higher on your list of priorities, Lower Town wins every time. Goodwick falls somewhere between the two.

There is evidence of people living on this section of the coast since prehistoric times, and the names of both Fishguard (a place to store or catch fish) and Goodwick (good bay) derive from the old Norse. But it was really only with the growth in modern transportation — both the port and the railway — that Fishguard began to prosper. At first, development centred on the traditional quay and fishing village of Lower Town. The growth in the size of vessels during the nineteenth and early twentieth centuries, and the coming of the railway to Goodwick in 1899, saw activity move slightly further north and west.

Lower Town and the old harbour at Fishguard

The route: **Fishguard (Lower Town) to Pwll Deri**

1 Section three starts at the entrance to the car park on the western side of the road bridge across the **River Gwaun** in Fishguard's **Lower Town**. Enter the car park and, passing to the right of an old warehouse, make your way towards a small building beside the harbour and then turn left along a surfaced path. Climbing the lane from the old harbour, past a couple of old lime kilns almost hidden by dense vegetation, take the next turning on the right — **Bank Terrace**.

At the end of the row of cottages, the lane becomes a narrow path. Keep left at a fork and then turn right on reaching a wider path.

Partially wooded and with the sea directly below, this path, known as the **Marine Walk** and bypassing most of modern Fishguard, makes a lovely start to the day. As you gain height, you get a great view across to Dinas Island from the previous section of the route; then, as you round a corner, you can see the enormous breakwaters of Fishguard's twentieth-century harbour. There are plenty of benches along the path should you wish to sit and admire these views.

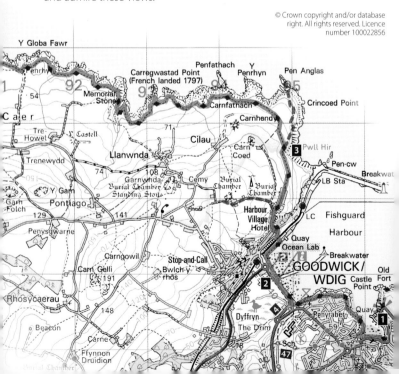

Safe haven: *The pretty eighteenth-century harbour at Fishguard's Lower Town*

Ignore any turnings to the left and, eventually, the surfaced path goes over to paving stones and passes **St Theresa's Rest Home**. Just before you reach the main road, drop down the steps on the right. At the bottom, swing right, passing **Bridge Cottage** and then picking up a walkway beside the beach.

This is **The Parrog**, the relatively undeveloped area that separates Fishguard and Goodwick. 👁 **Art, murals and mosaics** along the path depict scenes from local history.

2 On reaching a **small shelter** with murals on its internal walls, the path splits. Bear right here and follow the path into **The Parrog car park**, home to **public toilets**, a **café** and **tourist information**. Pick up a path beside the harbour wall and follow this to the right of the ferry terminal and beside the fenced port area. This fenced area is then crossed via a metal bridge. Turn right at the top of the steps on the other side.

After about 120 metres along this lane — just as the **Fishguard Bay Hotel** appears — go through the gap in the wall on your left.

The Fishguard Bay Hotel was once the home of a well-known local merchant — and likely smuggler — William Rogers. The Fishguard Bay Railway and Pier Company bought it in 1896 and, two years later, converted it into a luxury hotel for the nearby port's wealthy trans-Atlantic passengers. Under the management of Great Western Railway, a 40-bedroom hotel, complete with crystal chandeliers, marble fittings and terraced gardens, was created. The hotel was known then as the Wyncliffe.

A zig-zagging path climbs gently through the trees. Turn right at the road and follow this to its far end, ignoring a track up to the left.

Detour: *To the Garn Wen burial chambers*

The track curves uphill to the left to visit three Neolithic burial chambers scattered across the Garnwnda hillside.

On the **official route**, the houses along this road, part of **Harbour Village**, were built for railway men and the workers employed to construct the modern harbour's breakwaters. Sadly, some prehistoric burial chambers were destroyed during the building of the homes: only Garn Wen remains.

Finally saying farewell to the scattered settlements of Fishguard, you set out on a path that starts just to the left of a **solitary cannon**. Go through a gate and turn sharp left, keeping close to the hedgerow on your left.

3 The coastal path goes through a kissing-gate, missing out the tip of Pen Anglas.

Detour: *To the end of Pen Anglas headland*

The view from the end of this largely National Trust-owned headland overlooks six-sided basalt columns similar to those of Northern Ireland's Giant's Causeway.

Keeping to the **official route,** the coast path follows a broad, grassy swathe cutting through tall gorse bushes. After passing the walls of an old building on the left, you reach a fingerpost. Turn right here. There are more ruins among the dense vegetation on your left here.

A kissing gate on the coast path at Pen Caer

Last invasion: *The Carreg Goffa memorial commemorates the landing of French troops in 1797*

The geology of the cliffs has altered again today: the dark sedimentary and metamorphic rocks that form the higher, often jagged coastal features to the north and east of Fishguard have largely been replaced by lighter-coloured, more blocky cliffs formed from volcanic activity. Later, on Strumble Head, watch for exposed pillow lava. These pillow-shaped rocks are formed as a result of the rapid cooling of underwater lava eruptions. Inland, exposed rocky tors are strewn along the skyline — all the way from Garnwnda in the east to Garn Fawr in the west.

This area, known as **Pen Caer,** has been settled for millennia. Looking south from the coast path, walkers can see one or two loose clusters of homes, as well as a number of well scattered farmhouses. The landscape is dotted with small enclosures divided by banks of earth and stones, often covered in gorse. Some of these field systems are medieval, but, in a few cases, the boundaries have remained unchanged since the Iron Age. Prehistoric sites on the peninsula include standing stones, flint-working sites, a round barrow, a chambered tomb and Iron Age forts. There are also several early Christian sites and some medieval settlements.

After crossing a boggy area via **stepping stones**, the trail becomes a little less obvious, but don't be tempted by the footpath off to the left. The coastal path continues to weave its way around the coves and headlands of this gorgeous coast. There are a few dips to climb in and out of as you progress ever westward, but they're not as steep-sided as on previous days.

Sailors' friend: *Sunset at Strumble Head lighthouse from the cliffs above Carreg Onnen Bay*

The first drop to valley level is at **Cwm Felin**, a wooded gorge with a bridge in the bottom of it — and one of the few places where you will see trees today. Climbing out of Cwm Felin, turn right at a waymarked path junction and then continue uphill to the 👁 **Carreg Goffa memorial**.

The Carreg Goffa memorial was erected in 1897 to mark the 100th anniversary of the last landing of foreign forces on British soil. The so-called last 'invasion' took place on February 22, 1797 when 1,400 French troops led by Irish-American Colonel William Tate came ashore at Carregwastad Point. This was supposed to be part of a three-pronged attack by French revolutionaries in support of Irish Republicans. Tate's men didn't get far. Eight hundred of his 'Black Legion' were irregulars — mostly convicts and deserters. Discipline among this group quickly deteriorated and many of them abandoned the invasion, looting homes along the coast and, according to local legend, becoming sidetracked by a stash of alcohol that villagers had recently found on a shipwreck. There were a few minor skirmishes with local forces, but Tate was forced to surrender just two days after landing.

The heroine of the invasion was Jemima Nicholas, a Fishguard woman who,

armed with a pitch-fork, is said to have rounded up 12 of the would-be invaders. Another local story tells of how the French soldiers mistook local women, wearing traditional tall black hats and long red cloaks, for British Grenadiers.

After passing an idyllic white cottage at **Penrhyn**, wonderfully situated close to the cliff edge, you reach a junction of paths. Turn right here. The clifftop is increasingly rocky now with lichens and wildflowers adding a splash of colour to what might otherwise be austere surroundings.

Wildlife at Strumble Head

Strumble Head is a great place for spotting cetaceans and other marine life. Porpoises are particularly common all year round, but other visitors include basking sharks, orca and fin, humpback and minke whales. Risso's dolphins are seen from time to time, particularly mid-winter. Grey seals bask on the rocks around the base of the two tiny islands just off the coast — Ynys Onnen and Carreg Onnen. They can be heard barking at each other as they tussle for space on crowded rocks and beaches.

Briefly, nearing **Porthsychan**, the path comes away from the edge. It goes through a kissing-gate, bends sharp right to drop down the slope and then crosses a couple of small streams before reaching a bridge just above the secluded bay. Turn left after the bridge and then go through the kissing-gate on the right.

If you're finding all the gates on this section of the path a bit tiresome, just imagine how much worse it was when they were all stiles. There used to be a whopping 550 stiles on the Pembrokeshire Coast Path, each of them numbered. (The number plates still exist on some of the gateposts.) But, over the years, the stiles have been steadily replaced with gates for ease of access. Now there are only about 50 left.

As the lighthouse at **Strumble Head** first comes into view, bear right at a waymarked fork and then left at the next one.

4 Turn right along the road. In a short while, you get your first, tantalising glimpse of the next section of the route, including St David's Head. The road leads down to 👁 **Strumble Head lighthouse**, perched on top of a tiny island connected to the mainland by a short suspension bridge. The lighthouse is now fully automated and there is no public access to the island.

To continue on the cliff path, watch for a parking area on the left just as the road begins dropping steeply to the lighthouse. The path resumes here. The terrain now is different again: the path weaves its way through a landscape of

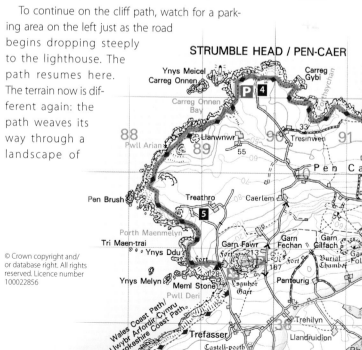

Distant views: *Looking across to the cliffs of Pwll Deri*

rocky, often heather-clad knolls of volcanic rock that have been rounded by glacial action.

After crossing a stile, the views of St David's Head in the distance come and go. In much the same way as Strumble Head has been the focus of attention for the past couple of days, this landmark will keep drawing the eye over the next two days. The path turns sharp left at the next waymarker post and climbs rocky ground to a high point that will stop you in your tracks. Now, for the first time, the dramatic cliffs of **Pwll Deri** appear — as does the whole of the coastline as far as St David's Head. It's a jaw-dropping moment.

5 The path passes around the top of the steep-sided cliffs of **Porth Maenmelyn**. Looking down into the void below is a vertiginous experience — with the ground plummeting more than 50 metres to the churning waters and dark, jagged boulders below. Yet, as you pass around the southern side of the bay, look back and you will see a set of dangerously eroded steps cut into the impossibly steep cliff-face: these were once used to gain access to the bay.

After crossing a stile just below **Pwll Deri youth hostel** — occupying probably the finest location of any Welsh hostel — you climb to the building's driveway. The hostel itself is down to the right, but the coastal path goes left to reach a quiet lane.

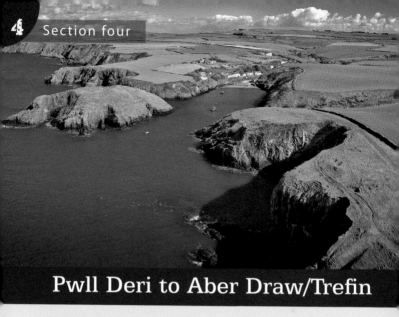

Pwll Deri to Aber Draw/Trefin

Distance: *16 kilometres / 10 miles* | **Start:** *Pwll Deri Youth Hostel SM 892 387*
Finish: *Mill ruins at Aber Draw SM 834 324* | **Maps:** *Ordnance Survey Explorer OL35
North Pembrokeshire, Landranger 157 St David's & Haverfordwest*

Outline: Less than wild as on previous days, but just as rewarding — as the
coast path continues along clifftops, past tiny beaches and tranquil coves.

Setting off from Pwll Deri means starting the day on a high — both literally
and figuratively. Surrounded by some of Pembrokeshire's most dramatic
coastal scenery, you head out along an airy, clifftop ridge. Beyond this, the
way drops in on the pretty, harbourside hamlet of Abercastle. Don't expect
a pub or café here though: the route may have lost its sense of remoteness,
but facilities are still scarce. The day ends at Aber Draw, just a few hundred
metres from the delightful village of Trefin.

Services: *Youth hostel at Pwll Deri. (Fishguard TIC: 01437 776636; fishguard.tic@
pembrokeshire.gov.uk.) There's a café at Tregwynt Mill, 1.1 kilometres off the main
route, but close to the high-water alternative. Public toilets in Abercastle. B&Bs, hostel,
campsite, toilets, pub and café in Trefin, 450 metres from the end of this section. Tony's
Taxis, St Davids: 01437 720931*

👁 **Don't miss:** Aber Mawr – sunken forest sometimes visible at low tide |
Castell Coch – Iron Age promontory fort on Penmorfa | **Carreg Samson** – Neolithic
burial chamber (300 metres off route)

▲ *Abercastle (Abercastell)*

Pwll Deri

Pwll Deri is the name given to the stunning bay located on the south-west edge of the Pen Caer peninsula. It is one of the most famous and most popular beautyspots on the Pembrokeshire coast, and is surrounded by some of the most dramatic coastal scenery encountered along the National Trail. Steep-sided cliffs, often with ominous-looking overhangs, stand tall above the crashing waves, while offshore are jagged stacks and partially submerged skerries, formed from the igneous rocks that stand up so well to marine erosion. Fulmars rise and fall on the air currents, effortlessly skirting the top of the wind-battered cliffs with barely a single flap of their wings, while all around wildflowers grow in colourful profusion. It's a truly atmospheric spot.

There are no facilities here, other than a small car park and the superbly located youth hostel — with its magnificent views out along the cliff-top ridge that runs south-west from Pwll Deri. The only other buildings are a few scattered farmhouses and white-washed cottages.

Above the hostel is the 213-metre Gawn Fawr, crowned by one of the many Iron Age hill forts along this stretch of the Welsh coast. Another, Dinas Mawr, sits directly below the hostel on a dome-like headland connected to the mainland by a narrow neck of land.

Looking back towards Strumble Head from the start of Day Four

The route: **Pwll Deri to Aber Draw/Trefin**

1 From the end of **Pwll Deri youth hostel**'s driveway, turn right and walk along the road for about 350 metres, passing a **memorial stone** along the way.

The stone is dedicated to the local writer Dewi Emrys, who lived from 1879 to 1952. The words at the bottom of the memorial are taken from his poem Pwll Deri, which celebrates the area and some of the local people. Dewi famously won the top prize, the Chair, at the National Eisteddfod on four separate occasions between 1929 and 1948, but poverty forced him to pawn one of his prizes.

Soon after the memorial, go through the small gate on the right — next to a fingerpost. Before long, you're back out on the clifftop again, following the broad crest of an easy, albeit sometimes rocky ridge that makes for excellent walking. You'll inevitably want to linger over this exhilarating, windswept section, enjoying the superb views, both back towards Pwll Deri, towered over by Gawn Fawr, and out along the coast towards St David's Head and the distinctive tor of Carn Penberry.

Coming down from the ridge, the path forks. Bear right here, although both paths eventually drop to the same gate — the left-hand branch simply cuts the corner. Having turned right at a fingerpost, you drop to a bridge.

Take a moment here to look to the right, to the steely grey cliffs of **Pwllcrochan**. Fearsome, razor-sharp arêtes lead off from the main cliff face leading to lumps of rocks that will, no doubt, one day become stacks. Some have already been undermined and have caves and arches cutting through them.

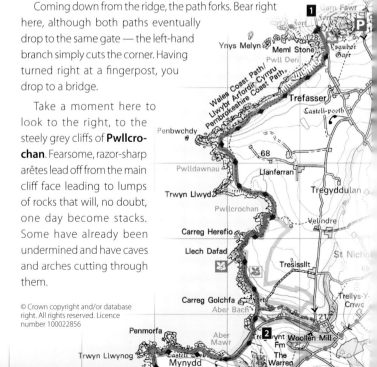

Breezy viewpoint: *Looking towards Penbwchdy headland from Garn Fawr, above Pwll Deri*

2 About 1.6 kilometres beyond Pwllcrochan, the next bay is **Aber Bach**. Fording the stream here is normally a straightforward undertaking, but if the water level is too high, you will have to follow a 1.8-kilometre detour inland (see 'high-water alternative' below). The main route goes right here, to cross the stream and then clamber over a massive, pebbly storm beach. On climbing out of the bay, bear right at the fork and continue along the cliff path.

> **Alternative high-water route**: *An inland route via Tergwynt Mill*
> Turn left just before the stream, following a path up through a pleasant, wooded valley, passing a few cottages along the way. At the road, turn right. (**Tregwynt Mill** and its small café can be reached by taking the lane on the left in a short while.) Take the next road on the right and, after about 700 metres, go through a small gate on the right. Bear left at a fork to regain the cliff path just above Aber Bach.

On the **official route**, you'll quickly reach the end of a minor road. This used to continue on towards Abercastle, but the sea has taken it. In fact, this is one of the fastest eroding sections of the Pembrokeshire coast, with the beach at Aber Mawr said to be moving inland at the rate of about a metre every year. Turn sharp right at the road-end to continue along the path, soon crossing the back of 👁 **Aber Mawr beach**.

Taking the plunge: Coasteering off the rocks near Aber Mawr

This rather unassuming spot has an interesting history, both in geological terms and from a human perspective. It very nearly ended up, not as the peaceful bay it is today, but as a bustling port and railway terminus. The great Victorian engineer Isambard Kingdom Brunel actually started work on building the railway in the late 1840s. In fact, evidence of this work can still be found in the dense vegetation behind the beach. Aber Mawr was supposed to form the western terminus of the South Wales Railway. A massive port was planned too, to handle trade with Ireland as well as trans-Atlantic traffic. However, in 1851, the work was abandoned after Brunel decided to build his port and railway terminus at Neyland on the Milford Haven waterway instead.

Marine sediments deposited by the Irish Sea ice sheet during the last glacial period are revealed in the cliffs of Aber Mawr as purplish-blue clays squeezed between layers of stonier material. Studying these deposits has helped geologists learn more about environmental conditions in Pembrokeshire during the late Pleistocene period. The substantial shingle bank at the back of the beach is often attributed to the massive storm of 1859, but it is more likely to be associated with rises in sea level that took place at the end of the last glacial period. The same is possibly also true of Aber Bach.

A submerged forest, dating back to about 6,000BC, is sometimes revealed here during particularly low tides or after storms.

Having crossed the beach, climb to a path junction and turn right. Keep right after the next gate. The path weaves a convoluted route around the edge of the high ground of **Mynydd Morfa**, allowing glimpses of secluded coves below, accessible only from the sea, and awesome, jagged cliff faces. Don't venture too close to the edge!

Prehistoric burials

👁 **Carreg Samson** *Neolithic burial chamber, or cromlech, is well worth the detour from the coast path. It is reached by following a signposted trail left as the cliff path climbs from Abercastle — about 300 metres off route. Built 5,000 years ago, it consists of an enormous capstone, almost 3 metres wide, resting on three of the upright stones below it. What visitors see today is just the exposed central chamber, which would once have been covered by a mound of earth.*

Narrow bay: *Looking back down into Abercastle as the coast path continues south-west*

👁 Castell Coch, *on* **Penmorfa**, *is just one of many dozens of Iron Age promontory forts along the Pembrokeshire coast, several of which are passed on this section of the route. The ditches and double embankments of the fort are just about visible. It also had an unusual zig-zagging entranceway that would've made it difficult to attack. A second* **Castell Coch**, *on* **Pen Castell-coch**, *is passed to the west of Abercastle.*

3 The next descent is into the sheltered bay of **Pwllstrodur**. Cross the bridge, turn left and then quickly swing right to climb again. After a gate, you are able to look down on the enormous boulders piled on either side of the bay.

4 Further on, you reach **Abercastle**, a lovely collection of cottages clustered around a long, narrow bay with the tiny island of **Ynys y Castell** standing guard in its entrance.

Abercastle, known in Welsh as Cwm Badau, or Bay of Boats, was once a busy trading port. Butter, corn and oats were exported to Bristol and Liverpool, while the main imports included anthracite and limestone. There is a well preserved limekiln on the sheltered, western side of the bay. The much larger ruin close to the mouth of the bay is an old grain store.

In August 1876, Abercastle became part of sailing history when Danish fisherman Alfred Johnson landed his small dory Centennial here, becoming the first person to cross the Atlantic single-handedly. It had taken him 66 days to sail from Massachusetts. A commemorative plaque near the slipway was unveiled in 2003.

On reaching the end of a lane close to a cottage, cross over and drop down the steps. Bear right at the fork and then walk beside a small stream, soon crossed via a stone bridge. Immediately in front of you now are some well-hidden **public toilets**, tucked around the back of the building. The path goes through the gate to the right of the building and skirts the southern side of the bay before climbing again.

Just after leaving **Abercastle**, you will see two trails on the ground: take the one nearer the cliff edge. The way ahead is less obvious beyond the next gate. As you swing around the top end of an old wall, try not to lose too much height; simply aim for the next wall straight ahead and then keep to the left of it over the next section of cliff. You lose the security of this wall after a gate. The path performs a sharp bend to the left here. The route is reasonably wide, but the crumbly nature of the edge is a little disturbing. You can see where sections of the cliff, undercut by the waves below, have slumped away.

5 A little more than 3 kilometres beyond Abercastle, you reach a fingerpost indicating a path to the left to **Trefin**. Those aiming for Trefin may wish to cut the corner here, but the main route continues to the right, soon passing some ruins and then dropping to **Aber Draw**. Cross the bridge over the stream close to the remains of the **old mill** and then head left to reach the road. While the coast path turns right along the road, those with their sights set on a bed in **Trefin** should turn left. It's about 450 metres from here to the village centre.

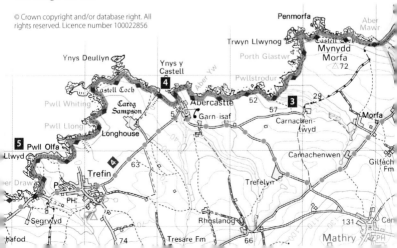

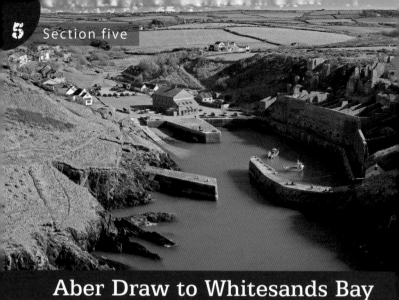

Aber Draw to Whitesands Bay

Distance: *18 kilometres / 11 miles* | **Start:** *Mill ruins at Aber Draw SM 834 324* | **Finish:** *Whitesands Bay car park SM 734 271* | **Maps:** *Ordnance Survey Explorer OL35 North Pembrokeshire, Landranger 157 St David's & Haverfordwest*

Outline: One final day on Pembrokeshire's wild, undulating north coast, taking in high cliffs, secluded settlements and atmospheric heathland.

The interesting settlements of Porthgain and Abereiddy are passed in the first few kilometres. After that, you've got 11 kilometres of reasonably tough and remote walking ahead of you. The sense of isolation grows the nearer you get to the open heathland of St Davids Head. This atmospheric headland, composed largely of volcanic rocks, is dotted with prehistoric remains and craggy little tor-topped hills. The day ends at Whitesands Bay, just a short bus journey from the delightful, tiny cathedral city of St Davids.

Services: *B&Bs, hostel, campsite, toilets, pub and café in Trefin, 450 metres from the start of this section. Pub, café and toilets in Porthgain. Seasonal snack van and toilets at Abereiddy. Campsite and bunkhouse, 400 metres off route at Pwll Caerog. Seasonal beach café, toilets and campsite at Whitesands. St Davids, 3 kilometres from the end of this section, has a range of accommodation, places to eat, shops, a chemist, and banks with cash machines. (St Davids Oriel y Parc Gallery and Visitor Centre: 01437 720392; info@orielyparc.co.uk.) Tony's Taxis, St Davids: 01437 720931*

Don't miss: Porthgain – interesting industrial ruins | **Blue Lagoon at Abereiddy** – disused quarry pit flooded by sea | **Coetan Arthur** – prehistoric burial chamber on St Davids Head

▲ *A gull's-eye view of Porthgain*

Aber Draw/Trefin

Trefin consists of a group of cottages, home to about 130 people, located on high ground just south of Pembrokeshire's northern cliffs. Its name comes from the Welsh 'Trefaen', meaning 'village on the rocky outcrop'. It's a charming spot, with a gentle, laid-back atmosphere that is reminiscent of the days before modern transport and television. Indeed, with no shops and only patchy mobile phone reception, walking into Trefin is a little like stepping back in time.

The nearby Aber Draw mill ruins make for a peaceful, if slightly melancholic spot. There's not much left of the mill now apart from its sad outer shell and a couple of millstones, but, for five centuries, this would have been a focal point for the community of Trefin. While the tiny bay below was busy with fishing boats and vessels laden with grain for milling, local people would bring sacks of wheat (for grinding into flour) or barley (to convert to winter feed for their livestock). The mill closed in 1918.

The site inspired one of Welsh poet William Williams's best known works: *Melin Trefin*. Williams, writing in the Welsh language, was better known as Crwys and was the Archdruid, or presiding official, at the National Eisteddfod from 1939 to 1947.

Mill ruins above Aber Draw's stony beach

The route: **Aber Draw to Whitesands Bay**

1 From the **mill ruins at Aber Draw**, head west along the road for about 200 metres. Close to a cottage entrance, go through a small gate on your right. As you head across the field, don't get too excited about the stone circle over to the right: having been created in the twentieth century, its origins are a lot less romantic than you might at first think. A faint path leads through a couple of fields, passing to the left of a prominent stone, before heading back out on to the clifftop proper.

After the next gate, the path cuts a few corners as it keeps a safe distance from the edge. Stay close to the fence/wall on the left. The route passes through one gap, but you shouldn't go through the second gap; instead, turn sharp right and then left, always keeping with the fence/wall. After another gate though, the path sticks more religiously to the cliff itself.

Watch for the substantial, grass-topped stack now separated from the mainland by a rock-filled chasm. This is **Ynys-fach***.*

A prominent **white obelisk** marks the start of the easy descent to 👁 **Porthgain**. After the gate on the edge of the tiny village, go right — down the gravel track.

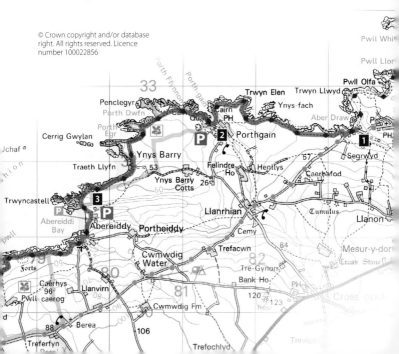

Sheltering arms: *Sturdy breakwaters protect Porthgain harbour against winter storms*

2 Dropping to the road, turn right to pass to the right of **The Shed**, a café and fish and chip restaurant housed in the former stone-works' machine shop. The public toilets are up to the left. Turn right along the western side of the **harbour** and climb the steps at the far end.

Scattered throughout Porthgain village and along the sides of the harbour are the industrial ruins of the nineteenth and early twentieth centuries. Exports included roofing slates from about 1850 until 1910, bricks from about 1890 until just before World War One and, later still, road stone. Enormous brick-built hoppers, used to store the crushed and graded granite for road building, still dominate the western side of the harbour. The works closed in 1931, and the Pembrokeshire Coast National Park Authority is now responsible for maintaining the structures left behind.

Soon after passing to the left of the remains of two stone constructions, the path splits. Bear left here; the lower path heads out to the disused works of **Penclegyr**.

*It was on the **Penclegyr headland** that granite was quarried for road stone. The line of a railway cutting and tramway as well as the remains of the winding house and smithy can still be seen out on Penclegyr. Those with a keen eye may also be able to trace out the route of the old trackbeds as well as the foundations of the weighbridge and other buildings associated with the stone-crushing plant on the clifftop east of the headland.*

Early lighthouse?: *Abereiddy Tower on the rocky headland of Trwyncastell and the Blue Lagoon*

Where the fence makes a sharp bend to the left, you will see a grassy trail heading out on to a long, narrow promontory, but the main path heads left, keeping close to the fence. Emerging on to a particularly exposed headland, you will see Abereiddy Tower.

This circular, stone-built construction is thought to date back to the eighteenth century. It's unclear what it was used for, although suggestions include a harbour entrance marker, a look-out and a rudimentary lighthouse.

The path comes away from the fence on this headland, but you need to watch for a low fingerpost where you bear half-left, crossing the grassy slope on a faint path. Eventually, you drop down some steps.

3 Turn left at the next path junction and then left again to go through a gate. Ignore the steps down to the beach on your right. Then, when the surfaced path bends sharp right, keep straight head, crossing the grass to a kissing-gate. (The public toilets are up to the left here.) Join a clear path from the left, cross a small bridge and then enter the car park at **Abereiddy**.

Slate quarrying at Abereiddy predates its development at Porthgain. Many of the ruins in the hamlet and to the north of the bay date from the 1830s. In the

*early days of the quarry, slate would have been shipped directly from Abereiddy,
but it was later moved, via a tramway, to the harbour at Porthgain.*

Detour: *To the Blue Lagoon*
A wheelchair-friendly path leads from the hamlet out to the 👁 **Blue
Lagoon**. Of course, the detour isn't compulsory for coast path wayfarers,
but if you do fancy a break from walking, the black sands of **Abereiddy
beach** might prove an interesting distraction: *trilobite and rare graptolite*

Blue Lagoon

*The Blue Lagoon at Abereiddy is a disused quarry
pit flooded by the sea in the early twentieth
century. The blasts and hammering are long
gone, replaced now by the screams of teenagers
as they take part in coasteering — leaping from
the cliffs and industrial remains into the calm,
blue waters below. In 2012, the Blue Lagoon was
the venue for a leg of Red Bull's world cliff-diving
championships.*

St Davids Head: *Coetan Arthur Neolithic burial chamber and Ramsey Island at sunrise*

fossils have turned up here, although they are more likely to be found in the cliffs and disused quarry.

From the beach car park on the **official route** at Abereiddy, walk up the road and then take the first road on the right. As you draw level with a two-storey house on your left, turn right through a small gate.

A little over half-way between here and the rocky beach at **Aber-pwll** are the earthwork remains of three Iron Age forts. The ditches, embankments and stony ramparts at **Caerau** are particularly well preserved.

A sign just beyond Caerau indicates a path to the bunkhouse and campsite at **Pwll Caerog**.

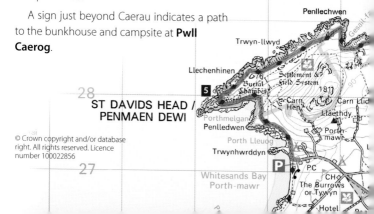

28

**ST DAVIDS HEAD /
PENMAEN DEWI**

27

4 This is soon followed by a steep, rocky drop to **two bridges** just above **Aber-pwll**. The climb out the other side is slightly easier, but be careful to bear left at the waymarker post at the base of the ascent.

Another ancient fort is passed at **Castell Coch**, *this one with a double ditch to defend the headland on which it stands.*

Before long, the crumbly cliffs associated with sedimentary rocks are largely replaced by harder volcanic formations. *A series of dramatic, rocky tors line up just inland from the cliffs: Carn Penberry, Carn Treliwyd, Carn Perfedd, Carnedd Lleithr and Carn Llidi. Formed from igneous intrusions into the softer sedimentaries, these proud sentinels have resisted much of the erosion and weathering that has befallen the softer surrounding rocks and now stand, island-like, above the surrounding land.*

You soon skirt the base of the first of these tors: **Carn Penberry**. Ever since rounding Strumble Head on day three, this distinctive hill has acted as a guiding influence, drawing walkers onwards to St Davids Head and another turning point on the National Trail.

Gull's-eye view: *Carn Llidi and the coast with Ramsey island just offshore*

Immediately after crossing a bridge at **Porth y Dwfr,** the path forks. The main route goes right, while the left-hand branch cuts the corner. The landscape, both coastal and inland, becomes considerably more rugged the closer you get to St Davids Head. As you make your way between rocky outcrops and piles of lichen-covered boulders, ignore any paths to the left, although hostellers may be interested in one of them — it points the way up to **St Davids Youth Hostel.**

Much of the St Davids Head peninsula is owned by the National Trust, which does an excellent job of protecting not only the precious habitats on this exposed section of the coast, but also the many prehistoric remains that lurk among the heather and bracken. Iron Age field enclosures are evident on the north-western slopes of **Carn Llidi***. Further west, the impressive* **Warrior's Dyke***, consisting of stone-built ramparts and ditches, cuts across the tip of the peninsula. On its seaward side are the Iron Age hut circles that it was built to defend. Probably the most striking of the ancient structures on the headland is* ☜ **Coetan Arthur,** *a burial chamber thought to be about 5,500 years old.*

Keep right at any forks in the path as you continue out to the far end of **St Davids Head**. There are trails all over the place here, but as long as you keep the sea close by on your right you can't go far wrong.

A **cairn** on the high ground provides superb views back towards Strumble Head and of the various islands lying off the coast. *The largest of these, Ramsey Island, will figure highly on the next section of the coast path. Further out to sea are the Bishops and Clerks, a group of small islands that have long caused navigational problems for boats. A lighthouse was built on South Bishop Rock, the most southerly of the islands, in the 1830s.*

5 Once you've reached the end of the peninsula, turn round and come back in along its southern side. Again, keep right at any forks. You should soon find yourself on a clear path skirting the southern flank of the high ground. It drops to cross a stream near the sandy beach at **Porthmelgan**. Steps climb beyond here. After a gate, you have an uninterrupted view of the long beach of **Whitesands Bay**, popular with surfers, kayakers and young sandcastle-builders. The path drops to the car park beside the beach, from where tired walkers can catch the regular shuttle bus into St Davids (summer only).

Looking back along Whitesands Bay

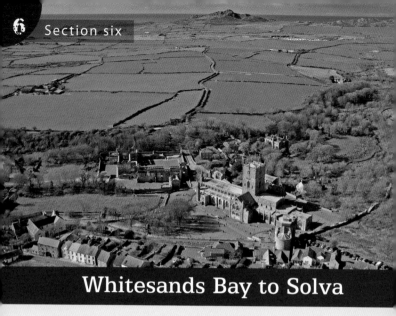

Whitesands Bay to Solva

Distance: *21 kilometres / 13 miles* | **Start:** *Whitesands car park SM 734 271* | **Finish:** *Solva harbour SM 805 243* | **Maps:** *Ordnance Survey Explorer OL35 North Pembrokeshire, Landranger 157 St David's & Haverfordwestt*

Outline: Having turned the corner of St Davids Head, the route changes as the wild north coast turns to sandy beaches, pretty coves and low cliffs. The remoteness of Pembrokeshire's north coast is lost beyond Whitesands Bay. From this long, sandy beach, the path follows a delightful section of coast that includes St Justinian's with its dramatically situated lifeboat station. Views of Ramsey Island dominate the early part of the walk, but after rounding Pen Dal-aderyn, it is the scene across the vast expanse of St Bride's Bay that commands attention. Should you wish to cut your day short, there are three points along the path where you can catch the bus into St Davids.

Services: *Seasonal beach café, toilets and campsite at Whitesands. St Davids, 3 kilometres from the start of this section, has accommodation, places to eat, shops, a chemist, and banks with cash machines. (St Davids Oriel y Parc Gallery and Visitor Centre | 01437 720392 | info@orielyparc.co.uk.) There are campsites at Caerfai Bay, Porthclais, St Justinian's and Nine Wells. Public toilets in Porthclais. Solva has pubs, B&Bs, public toilets and, in the upper village, a shop. Tony's Taxis, St Davids: 01437 720931*

Don't miss: St Davids – gorgeous cathedral and thirteenth-century Bishop's Palace | **St Justinian's** – dramatically located RNLI lifeboat station | **St Non's** – chapel ruins said to be birthplace of St David

▲ *St David's Cathedral and Bishop's Palace with Carn Llidi in the background*

St Davids

Although officially a city — the UK's smallest, in fact —  **St Davids** is, in terms of size and atmosphere, really just a large village. But it's a lovely village, with lots going on and, at its spiritual heart, the twelfth-century cathedral. This was built on the site of the sixth-century monastery established by St David, the patron saint of Wales — making it one of the oldest and most important Christian sites in the UK. St David is said to have been born at St Non's, which is passed on this section of the coast path, and was brought up at Llanon, near Trefin. Containing the remains of St David, the cathedral site became an important place of pilgrimage during medieval times with some of its more high-profile visitors including William the Conqueror, Henry II and Edward I.

Among the other notable features of the village-cum-city are the atmospheric ruins of the thirteenth-century Bishop's Palace, which was the area's main episcopal residence until the sixteenth century.

St Davids is not actually on the route of the National Trail, but because sections five and six complete a partial circuit of the city, never straying more than a few kilometres from its boundaries, it has become a major stopping point for long-distance walkers.

St Davids Cathedral and Bishop's Palace

The route: **Whitesands Bay to Solva**

1 Drop to the lower end of the car park at **Whitesands Bay** and bear left, passing in front of the lifeguard station. Climb gently through the dunes to a wide track along which you turn right.

Even as far back as the Bronze Age, Whitesands Bay was an important embarkation point for people travelling to Ireland. Traders, pilgrims and even saints crossed the Irish Sea from here. A chapel was built here in the sixth century to mark the spot where, supposedly, St Patrick set sail on his mission to bring Christianity to Ireland.

Take the path on the right, on the other side of a cottage. After the next sandy beach, don't be tempted by any paths to the left: these lead only into the campsites.

About 2.5 kilometres into the walk, as you round **Point St John**, **Ramsey Island** appears in its entirety.

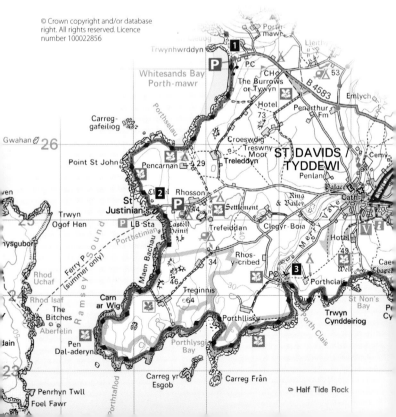

Saviours of the seas: *Steps lead down to the unusual lifeboat station at Porthstinian*

Clumps of ox-eye daisies, sea campion and thrift adorn the sides of the path as it eases its way round to 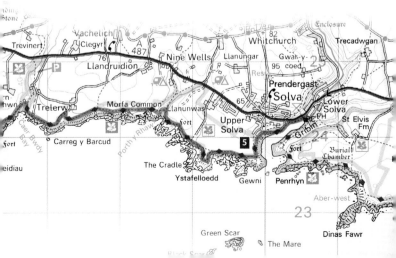 **St Justinian's**. An RNLI **lifeboat station** is picturesquely located in this narrowest of bays.

The chapel at St Justinian's, located on private land, is said to be the burial place of a sixth-century saint who lived on Ramsey Island. A Breton by birth, he was St

St Davids island: *Called Ynys Dewi in Welsh, Ramsey Island is a nature reserve owned by the RSPB*

David's confessor, but retreated to the island after growing disenchanted with the monastic community established at the cathedral site. Legend has it that he was beheaded after angering some of his followers. He then picked up his head and proceeded to walk across Ramsey Sound to the mainland.

2 Pass in front of a small shed containing the winding gear for a trolley that shifts equipment up and down to the lifeboat. Some steps lead down into the **tiny harbour,** but the coast path continues along the cliffs.

The tidal race here, combined with the influence of the reef just off Ramsey Island's east coast, known as The Bitches, makes the waters of Ramsey Sound an interesting place for boats. Large vessels avoid the area entirely, while kayakers come from far afield to pit their skills against its whitewater challenges. The tidal race can reach speeds of up to eight knots and, with the reef acting as a dam, there can be significant differences in the height of the water on either side of the rocks.

In 1910, the local lifeboat, Gem, came to grief on The Bitches after rescuing the crew of the ketch, The Democrat, during a gale. Powered by oars, the lifeboat was swept on to the rocks and smashed to pieces. Fifteen men managed to survive by clinging to the rocks, but three of the Gem's crew were killed.

As you pass above **Ogof Goch** and **Ogof Felen**, listen for the waves booming through the caves below. A little further on, a fenced-off mine shaft at **Penmaen Melyn** is all that can be seen of a copper mine, last worked in 1883.

Rounding **Pen Dal-aderyn**, the most westerly headland on mainland Pembrokeshire, marks another turning point on the route: with your back to Ramsey Island, the vast, open waters of St Bride's Bay stretch out ahead with Skomer Island clearly visible off Marloes Point, still several days' walking away.

Island life

Ramsey is Pembrokeshire's largest island — and the third largest in Wales. Its heathland and dramatic cliffs, up to 120 metres high in places, were bought by the RSPB in the early 1990s. Among the species that nest here are choughs, peregrine falcons and Manx shearwaters. The island's beaches and rocky bays are also home to a grey seal breeding colony. The only human residents are the wardens, but tourists can catch a boat from St Justinian's in the summer.

Safe haven: *The narrow harbour at Porthclais was once used to import coal and timber*

We are now on the tip of the **Treginnis peninsula***, home to the oldest rocks in Pembrokeshire. The volcanic rocks here, sometimes covered by younger sedimentaries, date back to the pre-Cambrian era, some 600 million years ago.*

The route winds its way between heather and gorse-covered rock outcrops, a favourite haunt of ponies and ravens. Keep right at any forks, unless the turning is clearly superfluous, just leading on to a headland and back again. You drop momentarily on to the beach at **Porthlysgi Bay**, but no sooner do your feet hit the pebbles than you turn sharp left up a track. This quickly narrows as it weaves its way along the cliffs.

The National Trust-owned headland here is composed largely of picrite, a relatively rare type of basalt after which the area is named.

Bear right at the next obvious fork, immediately after a gate. The path crosses an exposed section of cliff edge, from where you'll see an unusual arch cut into a stack. Rock pools fill the holes on the rocky shelf below. The path then comes some way inland to cross the inlet at **Porthclais**.

Porthclais is said to be the place where St David was baptised by St Elvis. Like Cwm Dewi near Dinas Island, the valley here was carved out by glacial meltwater during the last glacial period. The obvious difference between the two sites is that Porthclais was then flooded by rising sea levels when the ice sheets disappeared.

The harbour was built several hundred years ago, and imported coal and timber. At one point, the coal was used in the local gasworks. All that remains of the site, which closed in the early 1940s, is the old pump room. This now houses a seasonal kiosk run by the National Trust.

3 The path drops you at a lane close to a pair of **lime kilns** at the far end of the inlet. There are public toilets and a National Trust kiosk in the car park to the left here, but the coast path goes right. Cross the bridge and then turn right again on to the eastern side of the sheltered harbour. The way back on to the cliff is on the left just before the next pair of lime kilns. Ignore the path down to the right near the harbour mouth.

This is a sinuous stretch of coastline with curvy headlands and dark, semi-enclosed coves. On calm days, the kayakers who frequent these waters are able to explore the caves that cut into the base of the cliffs or paddle along the rock tunnels that slice through some of the narrower headlands.

The large grey house just above the path is St Non's Retreat. There is a modern chapel within its grounds, but it's also possible to visit the remains of an older
👁 **St Non's chapel**, *which is just 100 metres or so back from the cliff edge.*

Spring flowers adorn the cliffs above Caerfai Bay

Eroded rock: *A dramatic sea arch in a stack below the cliffs*

(Watch for the path to the left just before reaching the retreat.) The chapel is said to mark the birthplace of St David. It is named after his mother, who was a local aristocrat. His father, Sant or Sanctus, was a king of Ceredigion. Local legend states that the nearby spring, which miraculously appeared at the moment of St David's birth, has curative powers.

Keep right as you pass in front of the house.

4 As the path curves round **Caerfai Bay**, ignore a set of steps up to the left near a fingerpost. On a hot day, when the lure of a paddle in the cool sea proves irresistible, you may wish to take advantage of the turning on the right at the next fingerpost; otherwise, keep straight on at this path crossing.

You pass the grassed-over earthworks of an ancient fort on the headland that separates Caerfai Bay and Caer Bwdy Bay, but there is a finer example just beyond **Porth y Rhaw** in about 3 kilometres.

The path drops all the way to **Caer Bwdy Bay**, passing yet another lime kiln. *Sandstone from the quarry here was used to build St David's Cathedral and the Bishop's Palace. In 1998, it was briefly re-opened to provide stone for restoration work.* Turn right and immediately left after the concrete bridge at the bottom of the drop. Bear right at an obvious fork and then turn right at a waymarker post on the other side of a shallow dip.

A broad path cuts through the gorse along the flat top of **Morfa Common**. Just before the path starts dropping to the pretty, rocky inlet of **Porth y Rhaw**, look across the small bay to the ramparts of another Iron Age fort. The path passes right beneath this impressive site in a short while, but you get a better sense of the size and shape of the defensive position from this distance.

Soon after passing an impressive **arch in a large stack** — only visible if you step off the path — you get your first view of **Solva**. It's a lovely split village, part of which is built on the slopes above the sheltered harbour and part of which is clustered at the head of this delightful sun-trap.

5 After going through a gate, walk with a fence on your right. Bear right after the next gate. The path emerges on the driveway of a large white house. Follow this, and then take the next track on the right. At a junction of paths close to a bench, drop down the steps on your right. Turn left at the bottom, soon dropping on to the **quayside**, a busy little spot on a sunny, summer weekend. To stay on the harbourside path, keep right at two subsequent forks. This leads into the car park close to Solva's **Harbour Inn**.

Solva harbour from the air

Solva to Broad Haven

Distance: *18 kilometres / 11 miles* | **Start:** *Solva harbour SM 805 243* | **Finish:** *B4341 on northern edge of Broad Haven SM 861 138* | **Maps:** *Ordnance Survey Explorer OL35 North Pembrokeshire and OL36 South Pembrokeshire, Landranger 157 St David's & Haverfordwest*

Outline: A day of hidden, sandy coves and huge beaches, popular with surfers, all divided by sections of delightful cliff walking.

After several kilometres of cliff walking, this section is characterised by sandy beaches, large and small. Newgale Sands is the first: a 3 kilometre-long strand popular with surfers and other water sport enthusiasts. Nolton Haven, Druidston Haven and, finally, Broad Haven are the other main beaches encountered. With good road access to all but Druidston Haven, you're never too far from a café or ice-cream van. Each of the beaches and sandy coves is divided from the next by cliff paths providing excellent views across St Bride's Bay.

Services: *Solva has pubs, B&Bs, public toilets and, in the higher part of the village, a shop. (St Davids Oriel y Parc Gallery and Visitor Centre: 01437 720392; info@orielyparc. co.uk.) There's a café, pub, campsite and toilets at Newgale and Newgale Sands. Nolton Haven has a pub and toilets. There's a B&B at Druidston Haven. As well as a range of accommodation, places to eat and public toilets, Broad Haven has a shop with cash machine (fee payable) and a Youth Hostel. Tony's Taxis, St Davids: 01437 720931*

Don't miss: Solva – harbour and well preserved lime kilns | **Newgale Sands** – surfers' beach with a submerged forest | **'Teletubby House'** – grass-roofed eco-building at Druidston Haven

▲ *Solva from the sea*

Solva

You can't help but fall in love with Solva from the moment you first set eyes on it. As the coast path rounds the headland, its narrow harbour appears, hemmed in by steep, verdant hillsides. While small fishing boats and yachts bob up and down on its turquoise waters, white-washed homes stand on the high ground of Upper Solva. Lower down, colourful inns and cottages cluster at the waterfront.

Like the Gwadn valley running parallel with it to the south-east, the harbour here was formed when a glacial meltwater channel was flooded by rising sea levels after the last glacial period.

There is evidence of settlement in the area since the Iron Age when the narrow Gribin ridge had a fort on it, but it was in the early seventeenth century that the village really began to prosper. As a commercial port, its quaysides were home to several warehouses as well as no fewer than ten limekilns. The coast path passes several of these on its way out of the village.

The original Smalls lighthouse was built at Solva in 1776 before being shipped out and erected on a tiny cluster of rocks almost 35 kilometres off the coast.

Yachts face out to sea on the incoming tide at Solva

The route: **Solva to Broad Haven**

1 From the main harbour car park at 👁 **Solva**, head towards a bridge directly in front of a café called Thirty-Five. Once over the bridge, turn left and, almost immediately, go up the steps on the right, practically heading back on yourself. Bear right at a fork. The path soon drops to a set of well preserved **lime kilns** and then continues through the trees. *It passes a* **memorial** *that celebrates the donation of this headland to the National Trust in the 1930s by Richard Williams in memory of his father and grandfather.*

On reaching the delightfully airy, grassy ridge of **Gribin**, turn right and then, after just a few strides, go left to drop down the other side. At **Gwadn**, a bridge and a ridge of pebbles are crossed.

Like Solva's harbour, Gwadn was formed by the drowning of a glacial melt-water channel, but the anchorage here has long since silted up.

A rock out in the mouth of the bay and a National Trust farm about 1 kilometre up the valley are named after St Elvis, the sixth-century bishop who is said to have baptised St David.

The cliffs are very crumbly beyond Gwadn, so it is best to keep away from the edge. Some walkers may even choose to cut a few corners as the path weaves its convoluted way eastwards, but purists keen to stick with the official

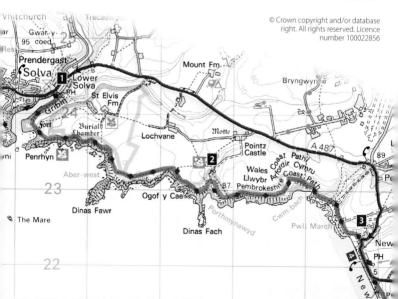

PEMBROKESHIRE COAST NATIONAL PARK/ 🅿
PARC CENEDLAETHOL ARFORDIR PENFRO

Distant views: *Walkers on the coast path above the northern end of Newgale Sands*

route — and those who appreciate this magnificent cliff scenery — should bear right at any forks encountered. Having said that, this 'keep-right-at-all-forks' rule does not apply when you reach **Dinas Fawr** where a trail heads out along the exposed spine of the headland, mined for lead and silver in the seventeenth century.

The cliffs between Gwadn and Newgale, almost 6 kilometres away, are reasonably high and the path keeps to the top for most of the way, only dropping a few times.

2 The first dip encountered is at **Porthmynawyd**. Turn right after the wooden bridge here and then bear left at the fork to climb again. There are another two small-ish dips before the path drops to a beach and then climbs more steeply. This ascent culminates in a superb view down the golden sands of the 3 kilometre-long beach at 👁 **Newgale**.

When sand and tidal conditions allow, a submerged forest sometimes appears at the northern end of Newgale Sands. This was first commented on by Gerald of Wales during a tour of the country in 1188. He wrote: "We then passed over Newgale Sands at which place a very remarkable circumstance occurred. The sandy shores of south Wales laid bare by the extraordinary violence of a storm, the surface of the earth, which had been covered for many ages, reappeared, and

Golden strand: *Dense gorse colours the back of the beach above Newgale Sands*

discovered the trunk of trees cut off, standing in the very sea itself, the strokes of the hatchet appearing as if made only yesterday. The soil was very black and the wood like ebony. This looked like a grove cut down, perhaps at the time of the deluge, or not long after."

There are many submerged forests like this along the Pembrokeshire coast, including at Abermawr, Whitesands Bay, Freshwater West, Lydstep and Amroth. Archaeologists have found flints and other tools close to several of these sites, showing they were inhabited. Clear evidence of the impact of rising sea levels, some of the submerged forests date back as much as 8,000 years. Rooted in peat below the sand, the tree stumps have been preserved by the constant presence of water. Over the centuries they have given rise to myths associated with Noah's flood — hence Gerald's reference to the "deluge" above — and ancient cities lost to the sea.

3 Turn right along the road at Newgale — passing a café, pub, toilets, phone box and campsite. If the tide is out, you can avoid much of the road walking by striding out along the compacted sand instead, but you'll have to come back up to the road before it climbs away from the shore.

Brandy Brook, crossed via **Newgale Bridge**, is generally regarded as the western end of the Landsker Line, the cultural and linguistic boundary between Welsh-speaking Pembrokeshire (to its north) and the English-speaking south.

Take the next road on the right, signposted to 'Nolton Haven'.

4 About 200 metres beyond the third toilet block since reaching the road at Newgale, watch for a small layby and fingerpost on the right. You pick

Death on the lighthouse

Thomas Howell and Thomas Griffith were early keepers at the Smalls lighthouse, Britain's most remote. When Griffith died during their watch, Howell feared he'd be accused of murder if he threw the body into the sea, so he put the body in a make-shift coffin and lashed it to an external balcony. The coffin soon began to disintegrate however, exposing Griffith's body. Howell had to put up with this grisly sight until the relief boat turned up weeks later.

up the cliff path again here. Bear left at the fork after the gate. At the next waymarker post, don't be tempted by a path off to the left.

On the cliffs between **Maidenhall Point** and **Nolton Haven**, we come across the first clearly visible signs of the Pembrokeshire coal field, which stretches from St Bride's Bay to Saundersfoot. The relatively thin seams, worked since the fifteenth century, produced high quality anthracite, which burned brightly without giving off too much smoke. As well as being used locally and throughout the UK, it was exported from Nolton Haven to France.

Dropping into a dip before Black Cliff, you'll see an old chimney, part of the engine house of a colliery that was opened in the 1850s and employed about 35 people. The last coal was dug here in about 1905, but mining in other parts of Pembrokeshire continued until 1950.

Druidston Haven beach at low tide

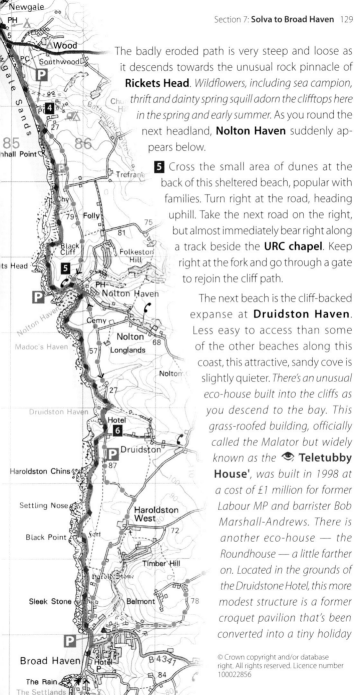

The badly eroded path is very steep and loose as it descends towards the unusual rock pinnacle of **Rickets Head**. *Wildflowers, including sea campion, thrift and dainty spring squill adorn the clifftops here in the spring and early summer.* As you round the next headland, **Nolton Haven** suddenly appears below.

5 Cross the small area of dunes at the back of this sheltered beach, popular with families. Turn right at the road, heading uphill. Take the next road on the right, but almost immediately bear right along a track beside the **URC chapel**. Keep right at the fork and go through a gate to rejoin the cliff path.

The next beach is the cliff-backed expanse at **Druidston Haven**. *Less easy to access than some of the other beaches along this coast, this attractive, sandy cove is slightly quieter. There's an unusual eco-house built into the cliffs as you descend to the bay. This grass-roofed building, officially called the Malator but widely known as the* 👁 *Teletubby House', was built in 1998 at a cost of £1 million for former Labour MP and barrister Bob Marshall-Andrews. There is another eco-house — the Roundhouse — a little farther on. Located in the grounds of the Druidstone Hotel, this more modest structure is a former croquet pavilion that's been converted into a tiny holiday*

Underground, overground: *The Malator House looks out to sea above Druidston Haven*

cottage. As well as solar panels and its own wind-powered generator, it has a reed bed drainage system for treating waste water.

Turn right at the bottom of the steps at Druidston Haven. You'll see two streams feeding on to the beach. Take the path rising between them, not the stepped path slightly further on. Turn right along the road.

6 About 150 metres after passing the entrance to the **Druidstone Hotel**, watch for a fingerpost on the right. This marks the start of an easy-to-miss path that runs parallel with the road before swinging half-right after a gate. Two more gates lead on to a surfaced path. Keep straight on here, ignoring the left turn. Where the surfaced path ends, you are able to look down on a series of rotational landslips known as the **Haroldston Chins** and **Druidston Chins**. (The coast path heads off to the left a few metres back from this viewing point.)

There is plenty of evidence between here and Broad Haven of the cliffs slowly slipping into the sea. If you stay with the main path at the next grassy fork, rather than cutting the corner by bearing left, you will see more examples of this, including the **Black Point Iron Age fort**. This is on a headland that has been sliding away since the 1940s. Keep to the landward side of any crevasses created where the cliff is becoming detached.

Bear right at the next waymarked path junction — through a gate. You later drop to a minor road close to the substantial beach at **Broad Haven**. Turn right here to reach a T-junction with the **B4341**, the main street through Broad Haven.

Unstable, banded cliffs near Haroldston Chins

Broad Haven to Marloes Sands

Distance: *20 kilometres / 12½ miles* | **Start:** *B4341 on northern edge of Broad Haven SM 861 138* | **Finish:** *Track leading to Marloes Sands SM 781 076* | **Maps:** *Ordnance Survey Explorer OL36 South Pembrokeshire, Landranger 157 St David's & Haverfordwest*

Outline: With lower cliffs and fewer visits to sea level than on previous days, this section, although long, makes for a relatively gentle walk.

Leaving the popular beaches of St Bride's Bay behind, this is a much quieter section of the National Trail. There's plenty of flora en-route, including a rare example of dense woodland clinging to the steep cliffs near Borough Head. Rounding Marloes peninsula, you finally turn your back on St Bride's Bay and end the day with a leisurely stroll above the spectacular beach at Marloes Sands. Marloes village is 1 kilometre inland from the northern side of the peninsula.

Services: *As well as a range of accommodation, places to eat and public toilets, Broad Haven has a shop with cash machine (fee payable) and a Youth Hostel. Accommodation, places to eat and toilets in Little Haven. Toilets at St Bride's Haven. B&Bs, campsite, pub and shop at Marloes, 1 kilometre off route. Martin's Haven has a campsite, toilets and seasonal information centre selling snacks and hot drinks. Youth hostel at Marloes Sands, 500m from end of this section. (Milford Haven TIC : 01437 771818 | milford.tic@ pembrokeshire.gov.uk.) Jock's Taxis, Milford Haven: 01646 698818*

Don't miss: Broad Haven – several interesting geological features on beach | **'Eyes of the Sea'** – 3 clifftop sculptures beyond Mill Haven | **St Bride's Haven** – pretty little thirteenth-century church

▲ *Broad Haven's huge sandy beach is popular with holidaymakers*

Broad Haven

Broad Haven doesn't have the long history of many of the towns and villages passed so far on the National Trail; in fact, it seems to owe its existence to the relatively modern phenomenon of tourism. It grew up as a seaside resort in the nineteenth century and remains a busy holiday destination today. Coast path walkers will find a decent range of facilities here.

The easy accessibility of its long stretch of golden sand, which holds a Blue Flag award, makes it one of the most popular beaches of St Bride's Bay. As well as being loved by families with young children who want to build sand castles and explore its rock pools, water sport enthusiasts find plenty to keep themselves busy here. Surf boards, paddleboards, kayaks and wetsuits can be hired from a shop in the village.

The northern end of the beach has a few interesting geological features, including some fine examples of folding: Den's Door, a stack with two arches in the base of it; and the Sleek Stone, an unusual, smooth tongue of rock jutting out into the sea, resembling, when viewed from above, a giant fish lying on its side.

Looking back along Broad Haven beach towards Den's Door

The route: **Broad Haven to Marloes Sands**

1 From the junction with the **B4341**, where you entered 👁 **Broad Haven** on the previous day, turn right to walk along the village's main street, passing a few pubs and the Londis shop. The road climbs Settlands Hill and then drops into **Little Haven**.

2 Turn right at the T-junction and head down to the delightful little cove, hemmed in by steep slopes on all but its seaward side. Formerly a harbour for exporting local coal, Little Haven has a lot more character and charm than its larger neighbour to the north.

Take the walkway on the far side of the bay, passing in front of the **Swan Inn**. Follow this almost all the way out to its end, but then, a few metres short of the viewing point, take the path on the left, soon climbing some steps. Bear right at the fork at the top to resume your cliff walking. The usual rule applies: unless otherwise instructed, keep right at any forks. Left-hand branches tend either to cut the corner or head inland.

Before long, you will see the woods on the relatively sheltered east-facing cliff of **Borough Head** — an unusual sight on the Pembrokeshire coast. Turn right along a minor road, but then, after just 80 metres, watch for a gate on the right, taking you back out on to the cliff. Bear left at a fork soon after entering the woods, a gorgeous combination of oak, beech and other deciduous species. *Even once you've left the trees behind, the cliffs are positively dripping with vegetation*

Stack Rocks

Howney Stone

Mill Haven

Halfway Rock

Warey Haven

Huntsman's Leap

St Brides Haven

Ripperston Fm

The Nab Head

The Falls

Tower Point

St Brides

Windmill Park

Castle

Eastfield Fm

when compared with much of the coast path. A burst of sun after a summer shower reveals the cliff's true verdancy, almost surreal in its depth.

The path continues past the scant remnants of a couple of Iron Age forts and a few intriguingly named inlets: **Brandy Bay, Dutch Gin** and **Foxes' Holes.**

3 Dropping to the delightful cove of **Mill Haven,** you'll see **Stack Rocks** a little way offshore. Turn right at the waymarker post to cross a bridge at the back of this red-cliffed bay.

Just beyond Mill Haven is a sculpture known as the 👁 'Waking Eye'. This is one of three pieces of work on this stretch of coast created by stone-carver Alain Ayers in the late 1980s.

St Bride's Castle forms a grand backdrop to the easy descent into **St Bride's Haven.**

4 Cross the rocks on the eastern side of this fabulous little bay, below **Cliff Cottage.** You can now either carry on

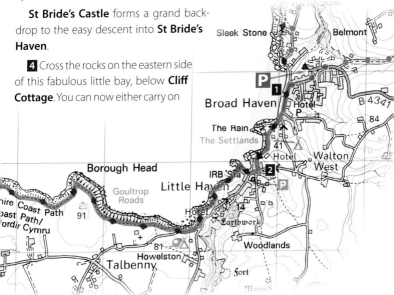

around the edge of the bay — passing the lime kiln and then picking your way across some more rocks — or you can use the trail up to the parking area and then take the path furthest right. Either way, you end up next to a sturdy wall: first you have it on your right and then you cross to the seaward side.

The 👁 church at St Bride's is dedicated to St Bridget, a nun who established several religious communities in Ireland. It dates from the thirteenth century and was probably built on the site of an earlier chapel. The stained glass windows in

Gateway to the islands: *Martin's Haven is the embarkation point for boats to Skomer*

the chancel and nave, as well as several other features in the building, were given by the Barons of Kensington, who lived, for a while, at St Bride's Castle.

The imposing mansion, first seen as the coast path descends to the bay, was built by the Phillips family in 1833 on the site of a mid-eighteenth century house called The Hill. It was bought by the fourth Baron Kensington in 1880, although death duties forced the family to sell it in 1920. From 1923 until 1978, the house was known as Kensington Hospital. In its early years, it specialised in treating children with tuberculosis. No doubt, the conditions experienced by the children back then were a far cry from those of today's residents — since 1991, the building and its 99 acres of parkland have been part of a luxury timeshare complex.

The coast path eases its way towards **The Nab Head**, once occupied by Mesolithic people. *Archaeological digs have revealed that The Nab Head was used 10,000 years ago, probably as a seasonal camp. Thousands of tools were discovered here, including microliths (tiny spearpoints), drill bits and tools used to scrape and clean skins. More than 600 perforated stone beads, possibly tokens of the owner's status that may have been traded, were also found.*

In summer, the west-facing cliffs beyond The Nab Head are a riot of colour: wildflowers cling even to the steepest of slopes in the most incredible manner.

After those first few tough days on the northern coast, this section of the route will feel relatively easy: the cliffs are low and there are only a few gentle dips to negotiate. The next one of these comes at **Musselwick Sands** where the path drops from **Black Cliff**. (At low tide, it's possible to access the deserted beaches here.) Take the path rising on the left, but make sure that, soon after a fingerpost, you turn right. The temptation here is to keep to the clearer path and head inland. Resist! Unless, of course, you want to go into **Marloes village**.

Martin's Haven near the far end of the **Marloes peninsula** is where day-trippers intent on visiting Skomer and other nearby islands catch their boat. This is your last real chance to look back across St Bride's Bay — all the way across to Pen Dal-aderyn, in fact — and enjoy that great sense of satisfaction that comes from looking back at a skyline and knowing that you've walked it all.

The National Nature Reserve of Skomer Island, managed by the Wildlife Trust of South and West Wales, is home to a wide variety of creatures. Puffins, Manx shearwaters, choughs, guillemots, razorbills and grey seals all breed here, while the surrounding waters are so rich in wildlife that they have been designated as one of the UK's four Marine Nature Reserves. In spring, the island is awash with bluebells, an indication that it was once covered in woodland.

5 After dropping down the steps into the bay at **Martin's Haven**, turn left along the surfaced track, soon passing the public toilets and a small Wildlife Trust shop that sells hot drinks and snacks. Watch for the inscribed

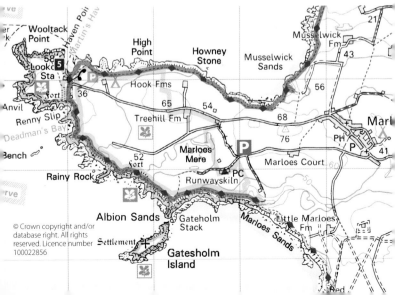

Tranquil inlet: *A typical Pembrokeshire lime kiln and cottages at St Bride's Bay*

Celtic ring-cross in the wall close to the converted fisherman's cottage. As the track swings left, go through the gap in the wall on your right to enter the so-called **Deer Park**. The coast path goes left after the kissing-gate — alongside the wall — but the more enthusiastic can head up the steep slope on the right and continue on past the old **Coastguard lookout station** to circuit this little headland.

The Deer Park is the name given to the far end of the Marloes peninsula. You won't see any deer here — and there's no evidence to suggest there ever were any — but you might see cattle and ponies. The old Coastguard lookout station is now manned by volunteers of the National Coastwatch Institution (NCI), a charity set up in 1994 to keep a watch for people in trouble along the UK's shores. About 3,000 years ago, the area was occupied by a fort, the ramparts of which can still be clearly seen on the ground.

Whether or not you decide to complete the circuit of the headland, you'll eventually leave the **Deer Park** via a kissing-gate. After the next bridge and gate, closely cropped turf makes for pleasant walking across the flat-topped cliffs above a series of small bays.

The island directly ahead is **Skokholm**. *The larger* **Skomer Island** *is over your right shoulder. The shoreline below is a jumbled mess of stacks and boulders of all shapes and sizes, twisted and torn by the elements.*

Just after crossing a tiny stream, there is a path to the YHA's **Marloes Sands hostel** on the left — close to yet another hillfort site, this one above **Victoria Bay**. Hostellers might prefer, however, to continue to another turning about one kilometre further along the coast path.

Gannets on Grassholm

Out beyond Skomer — about 13 kilometres off the coast — is Grassholm, another island reserve, this one owned by the RSPB. Wales's most westerly point, Grassholm is home to 39,000 pairs of noisy, smelly gannets, making it the third largest breeding colony in the UK, supporting around 10 per cent of the world's population. Boat trips run throughout the summer, weather permitting, but visitors are not allowed to land.

Marloes Sands to Sandy Haven

Distance: *21 kilometres / 13½ miles* | **Start:** *Track down to Marloes Sands SM 781 076* | **Finish:** *Lane at Sandy Haven SM 853 075* | **Maps:** *Ordnance Survey Explorer OL36 South Pembrokeshire, Landranger 157 St Davids & Haverfordwest*

Outline: After rounding a rugged headland, the path makes its way towards the Milford Haven waterway, crossing an estuary along the way.

From Marloes Sands, the path winds its way around the Dale peninsula, all the way to St Ann's Head — another section of superb cliff and coastal landscape. The route then drops to Dale, where walkers can rest and watch windsurfers and sailors enjoying the sheltered waters. The small estuary here is easily crossed at low tide, but the high-tide alternative adds 3.4km to the total distance. A winding cliff-top route then leads to gorgeous Sandy Haven, a sylvan hideaway surrounded by luscious woods.

Services: *Youth hostel at Marloes Sands, 500 metres from the start of this section. Café, pub, B&Bs, small shop and toilets in Dale. B&Bs and campsite at Sandy Haven, but the nearest places to eat are the pubs in St Ishmael's and Herbrandston. (Milford Haven TIC: 01437 771818 | milford.tic@pembrokeshire.gov.uk.) Jock's Taxis, Milford Haven: 01646 698818*

Don't miss: Cobbler's Hole – fascinating rock formation at St Ann's Head | **West Blockhouse Fort** – built in 1850s to guard against French attack | **Pickleridge lagoons** – important for overwintering birds

▲ *Wales Coast Path fingerpost at Marloes*

Marloes Sands

Marloes Sands is the name given to an almost 2 kilometres-long beach that stretches from Gateholm Island in the west almost all the way to the edge of the disued Dale airfield in the east. This fabulous sweep of golden beach is littered with boulders and rocky pinnacles thrusting up through the sands, giving it a slightly surreal feel. It may have been this other-worldly quality that led to it being used to film scenes for the 2012 fantasy Snow White and the Huntsman.

The cliffs behind the beach are made up largely of red sandstone and grey shale, formed about 420 million years ago. One of Marloes Sands' most distinctive features is the Three Chimneys formation: three lines of alternating sandstone and mudstone lifted into a vertical position by a collision of continents almost 300 million years ago and then weathered in such a way that the harder sandstone layers stand out from the cliff like giant book-ends.

Just over a kilometre inland of the beach is the small but uninspiring village of Marloes. With B&Bs, a pub, campsite and small shop, it might prove a useful stopping place for walkers who want a little more than the Marloes Sands youth hostel can provide.

Marloes Sands is a popular family beach in summer

Sundown: *Marloes Sands lit by the setting sun, with Skomer on the horizon*

The route: **Marloes to Sandy Haven**

1 From the track leading down on to **Marloes Sands**, cross the small bridge and climb the steps back up on to the cliff. (Alternatively, if the tide is out, you can drop on to the beach and walk east along it to the next set of steps. It's only a few hundred metres, but it'll give you a taste of this fantastic beach, one of the best in Pembrokeshire.)

The concrete tracks first encountered as you pass the far end of the beach are the remains of Dale military aerodrome. *Nowadays, you won't see any of the Wellington bombers that Polish airmen flew from here during World War Two, just a few sheep grazing.* Drop into a dip to pass to the right of a fenced group of cottages**, The Hookses** — an unexpected sight on this otherwise lonely stretch of coast. Climbing out the other side, head straight back on to the clifftop; don't be tempted by the old path that cuts straight across the face of it.

2 As you drop towards **Westdale Bay**, you will catch your first glimpse of the estuary at Milford Haven. It's on the other side of the **Dale peninsula** to your left. Some walkers, keen to catch low tide at **Dale** and avoid the lengthy

detour inland, choose to cut across the neck of the peninsula here and miss out St Ann's Head. To do this, you'll need to go through the gate on the left just after passing the beach access steps. For those determined not to cut corners, continue on the cliff path.

The first site of interest passed on the next stretch of coast is the Iron Age fort on Great Castle Head. Below, the sea is littered with small jagged stacks and islets, almost black on dull days, but gloriously red when the sun is shining. Further

Tanker disaster

On February 15, 1996, the Sea Empress oil tanker ran aground off St Ann's Head, at Milford Haven. Over the next few days, as attempts were made to refloat the stricken vessel and its hull was repeatedly gouged open, about 72,000 tonnes of crude oil poured into the sea. It took 12 months to clear the oil from a 200 kilometre stretch of coastline but many thousands of birds died and local breeding stocks of fish and shellfish were badly depleted.

south is another fort at Little Castle Head. Just inland of this is the National Trust property of Kete. Although nothing remains today, there were hundreds of small buildings here in the middle of the twentieth century — all part of the Royal Navy's Aircraft Direction Centre and School of Meteorology. After closure in 1960, the buildings were totally flattened.

Seaside rock: *The modern lighthouse perched on the red and grey striped cliffs on St Ann's Head*

The path eventually winds its way to the buildings huddled around the lighthouses at St Ann's Head.

3 Turn right along the lane, keeping right when it forks, and you'll soon pass to the left of the **old lighthouse**, which was later converted to a Coastguard station. On reaching the large gate to the newer (1841) lighthouse, the main route goes left, although the path to the right is well worth the short detour to see the double folding in the old red sandstone of 👁 **Cobbler's Hole**.

Having gone left at the 'new' lighthouse, follow the fence on the right. As you draw level with the last in the row of cottages on the right — there is a fingerpost here — turn sharp left. A waymarker post in the middle of the field helps you find your way down to a wooden gate, beyond which the path is more obvious again. It soon drops to **Mill Bay**.

This unassuming spot played a key role in a major turning point in British history. It was here, in early August 1485, that the 28-year-old Henry Tudor landed with a small army of about 1,800 French mercenaries. Henry then marched across Wales and England, gathering an army totalling about 5,000 and subsequently defeated Richard III in the Battle of Bosworth Field in Leicestershire. This was the last major confrontation in the War of The Roses, the civil war between the Houses of Lancaster and York, and Henry's victory for the Lancastrians marked the start of the Tudor dynasty. He was now King Henry VII.

Guns and sail: *Dale Fort guarded Milford Haven from French warships during the Napoleonic Wars*

Mill Bay may seem like an unlikely spot to begin a major military campaign, but this was home soil for Henry. Although he'd spent most of his life in exile in France, he'd been born in nearby Pembroke Castle, so he had plenty of supporters in the region. And choosing a secluded spot like Mill Bay allowed his men to come ashore unopposed. It is claimed Henry later built a chapel on St Ann's Head, close to the site of the modern lighthouse, to give thanks for his safe landing in Wales.

Back on the cliff, the continuing path isn't obvious at first, but as long as you keep close to the fence on the right for now, you won't go wrong. The route later crosses to the seaward side of the fence and then reaches the **West Blockhouse Beacon**, which is used as a navigational aid for ships entering Milford Haven. Cross straight over the track here.

 West Blockhouse was the site of one of the two defensive structures built by Henry VIII in 1539 to protect Milford Haven from attack by the Spanish. Nothing remains of the structure at West Blockhouse, although there are some Tudor remains at East Blockhouse on the Angle peninsula on the eastern side of the waterway. *The fort that can be seen today at West Blockhouse was built in the 1850s to guard against attack by the French. This was then restored in time for World War One, although it wasn't until World War Two that the guns that had guarded this strategic location for centuries were first*

fired in anger — at the German aircraft bombing Pembroke Dock. The fort was later bought by the Landmark Trust, who restored it and now rent it out as one of their rather quirky holiday lets.

The path on this eastern side of the peninsula is more undulating — and, in the summer, more overgrown — than on the easy-going western edge. And, while your gaze would inevitably have been drawn to the misty blue horizon on the other side, it is the industrial complexes of the estuary that now dominate the view.

Go straight over at a crossing of paths above **Watwick Bay** and then turn right immediately after a small gate. Having crossed a footbridge in **Castlebeach Bay** and climbed through the trees, you reach a grassy crossing of paths close to **Dale Point**. Bear left here to drop to a quiet road.

The road to the right here leads to Dale Fort Field Centre. *Run by the Field Studies Council to help young people enjoy and understand the area's natural environment, it occupies another of the forts built in the middle of the nineteenth century to protect Milford Haven from attack by Napoleon III.*

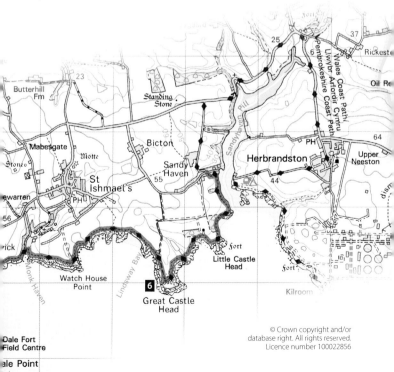

4 The coast path goes left along this road. Keep right on reaching a road junction in **Dale**. After passing a pub, public toilets and café, turn right at a T-junction.

Now a quiet spot that's home to a small sailing club, Dale was one of Milford Haven's most important fishing and trading ports in Tudor times. Ship-building continued here until the 1850s.

The road passes beside the beach and then climbs out of the village. For three-and-a-half hours either side of low tide, it is possible to cross the estuary at The Gann without getting your feet wet.

5 If you have hit upon the crossing at the right time, you will find the path on the far side of the parking area just after passing a pair of **lime kilns**. It heads out across the **Pickleridge causeway**.

*This long shingle ridge was deposited when the last ice sheets began melting. Marshland subsequently formed inland of it. During World War Two, large quantities of sand and gravel were dug out to build airfields, including the one at Dale. This left substantial pits. These saltwater lagoons — the 👁 **Pickleridge lagoons** — are now an important habitat and are protected as a Site of Special Scientific Interest. It is particularly important for over-wintering birds.*

The tidal crossing over The Gann

Artist's delight: *A high estate wall backs secluded Monk Haven bay*

Beyond the causeway, the coast path crosses the narrow channel via a small bridge and some stepping stones. Once over this and a ridge of rough ground, pick your way along the beach for about 650 metres — until you see a fingerpost directing you up a path on the left. Turn right after the gate at the top. (To avoid the beach, follow the track uphill just after the ridge of rough ground to join the high-tide alternative.)

High-tide alternative: *An inland loop avoiding the beach*
Continue along the road, finally crossing the estuary's stream via **Mullock Bridge**, almost 3 kilometres north of Dale. About 500 metres beyond the bridge, you will see **Mullock House** on your left. Soon after this, turn right along the driveway of **South Mullock.** Take the shady path to the left of the cottage and then walk down the side of the field, keeping close to the fence on the left. This swings round to a gate. Cross a muddy area and a bridge before going through another gate. A faint trail leads through the long grass, again keeping close to the hedges on the left. The next gate provides access to a fenced path. At the top of this, turn left and immediately right. Turn right on nearing the abandoned farm buildings at **Slate Hill** and then go left as you enter a field. Go through the wooden gate next to the double farm gate at the bottom of the field and turn left. (Those who crossed the estuary

but decided against the beach walk join the high-tide alternative here.)
Turn right along a surfaced lane and then go left at the bottom, rejoining
the main coast path.

Back on the **official route**, pass to the left of a farm building and then go
through two small gates in quick succession. From the low cliffs, you can see
across the mouth of the estuary to the Angle peninsula — more than two
days' walking away. Keep right at a path junction close to a high wall at **Monk
Haven**. This substantial eighteenth-century construction marks an old estate
boundary. On the other side of it is the tiny, but peaceful **Monk Haven bay**.

Climbing through the trees on the other side, turn right again at the next
crossing of ways. The **ruined tower** on the cliff in a short while is part of a
Victorian folly.

The towers, jetties and other paraphernalia of the oil refineries are far
enough away to be relatively unobtrusive at this stage: they don't yet detract
from the delights that this section of coast still has to offer. These include the
gorgeous, hidden bays at **Watch House** and **Lindsway**, first spotted after
the path passes some defensive structures left over from World War One.
The cliffs here, higher and steeper now, are clothed in green to within a few
metres of the water's edge. It is possible to access the beach at **Lindsway
Bay** by dropping down a steep flight of steps just after passing a path to 'St
Ishmael's' on your left.

6 Nearing the radar station at **Great Castle Head**, you come upon a path
junction. Turn right along the track and then, just before a white building,
take the grassy path on the left, running alongside the grassed-over ramparts
of an **Iron Age fort**.

Crossing the red cliffs of **Butts Bay**, the path emerges close to the **Little
Castle Head beacon.** Turn right here. The path winds its way across the
cliffs and along field edges before entering woodland that is awash with the
yellow of primroses in early spring. You eventually drop to a quiet lane at
Sandy Haven. The low-tide route and the high-tide alternative diverge here.

Pembrokeshire Coast National Park Ranger and walkers on Abereiddy beach

The National Trail

Behind the scenes

Like Rome, the Pembrokeshire Coast Path wasn't built in a day; in fact, it took 17 years to complete. The route was first surveyed in 1953, the year after the National Park was established. With the easy bit done, the next job was to negotiate hundreds of new rights-of-way with landowners. Then came the path-building, construction of bridges, erection of fingerposts, and siting of stiles... Finally, on May 16, 1970, the Pembrokeshire Coast Path was officially opened.

Yet the opening of the path was only the start. A lot of work goes on behind the scenes to ensure walkers have as enjoyable and safe an experience as possible. With funding from Natural Resources Wales, the National Park Authority looks after path maintenance. The National Trail Officer walks the entire route once a year to check its condition. From this, a programme of repairs and renewals is drawn up, with most of the work completed during the winter. In summer, the wardens cut back vegetation encroaching on the path. They also carry out urgent repairs: reinstating bridges wrecked by storms, repairing damaged gates, removing fallen trees... The list is endless.

More information: There's a section devoted to the Pembrokeshire Coast Path on the National Trails website – www.nationaltrail.co.uk

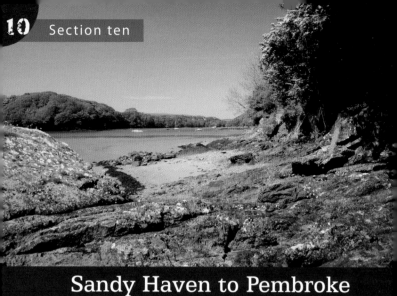

Sandy Haven to Pembroke

Distance: *27 kilometres / 17 miles* | **Start:** *Lane at Sandy Haven SM 853 075*
Finish: *Northern side of Mill Bridge, Pembroke SM 983 016* | **Maps:** *Ordnance Survey Explorer OL36 South Pembrokeshire, Landranger 157 St David's & Haverfordwest*

Outline: A short walk on low cliffs is followed by long sections through the towns beside the Milford Haven waterway as well as some woodland. Having started the day with a crossing of pretty Sandy Haven Pill (tides permitting) and a stroll along the cliffs, we enter new terrain. This next section, past two sprawling LNG sites and through small towns can look tedious on the map. In reality, the coast path bypasses the ugliness. Indeed, there are pleasant surprises, including gorgeous woodland, promenades and gardens, sparkling marinas and pretty waterfronts. (**N.B.** If the tide is in at Sandy Haven, the alternative route via Herbrandston adds 6 kilometres to an already long day.)

Services: *B&Bs and campsite at Sandy Haven, but the nearest places to eat are the pubs in St Ishmael's and Herbrandston. (Milford Haven TIC | 01437 771818 | milford.tic@ pembrokeshire.gov.uk.) There are lots of places to eat, sleep, buy provisions and access cash machines on this section, including Hakin, Milford Haven, Hazelbeach, Neyland, Pembroke Dock and Pembroke. Public toilets at Gelliswick Bay, Milford Haven, Hazel- beach, Pembroke Dock and Pembroke. Launderettes in Milford Haven and Pembroke Dock. Jock's Taxis, Milford Haven | 01646 698818*

Don't miss: Cleddau Bridge – massive road bridge over the waterway | **Pembroke Dock** – buildings and defences associated with 19th-century dockyard | **Pembroke Castle** – substantial Norman remains

▲ *Sandy Haven seen from the rocky shore*

Sandy Haven

Sandy Haven is a serene spot: a collection of lovely cottages and farms hidden away in lush deciduous woodland that hangs over the banks of Sandy Haven Pill. Depending on the state of the tide, the pill — or creek — alternates between a broad gulf and a narrow trickle of water, easily crossed by a small footbridge and stepping stones. When the tide is out, small yachts and motor boats sit patiently, marooned on the mudflats while a dark line on the low cliffs indicates the high-water mark. When the sea returns, the crossing disappears and it's hard to imagine getting to the other side without the aid of the ferry that once existed here.

The main beach at Sandy Haven is backed by low-lying cliffs of old red sandstone. This area is experiencing one of the fastest rates of erosion along the Pembrokeshire coast, causing the National Trail to be moved inland four times since 1989.

Bed and breakfast accommodation is available in Sandy Haven and there is a campsite on the eastern side of the pill, but there are no other facilities. Herbrandston, close to the end of the high-tide alternative route and about 1.5 kilometres off the main route, has a small shop and pub.

Lush woods frame Sandy Haven Pill at low tide

The route: **Sandy Haven to Pembroke**

1 Having dropped on to the lane at **Sandy Haven**, turn right for the low-tide route, passable for about two-and-a-half hours either side of low tide. The lane drops to the shore. Cross the **bridge and stepping stones** and then make your way across the mud banks. Turn right up the slipway in front of the white cottage, known as **Ferry Cottage**. When the lane swings left, go through the gate on the right. (Those forced to take the high-tide alternative rejoin the main route here.)

High-tide alternative: *Inland route avoiding the shore*

Turn left after dropping to the lane at **Sandy Haven** and then take the road on the right, just opposite a lime kiln. Turn right at the T-junction — signposted 'Milford Haven' — and then follow this road all the way to **Herbrandston**, crossing **Rickeston Bridge** and **Clay Bridge** along the way. (About 350 metres beyond Clay Bridge, watch for a permissive path on the right. Keeping to field edges, this runs parallel with the road for about 600 metres.) Where the main road bends sharp left on the edge of

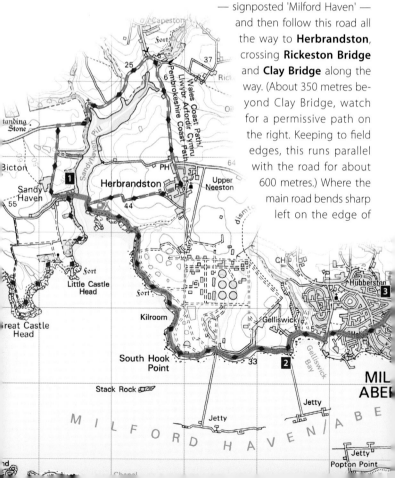

In times of peace: *A Palmerston fort on Stack Rock, off South Hook Point*

Herbrandston, turn right. Take the path on the right beside **St Mary's Church Hall**. After crossing a field, turn right along a lane that soon drops towards **Sandyhaven Pill**. Close to the estuary, as it swings right, go through the gate on the left to rejoin the main route.

The **official route** soon leads up into a static caravan site where you join a track. When this peters out, drop to a gate in the corner. After two more gates, you're back on the cliffs. Ignore the steps dropping down on to the beach in a short while, but then bear right at the next fork.

Just off **South Hook Point** *is* **Stack Rock**, *a small*

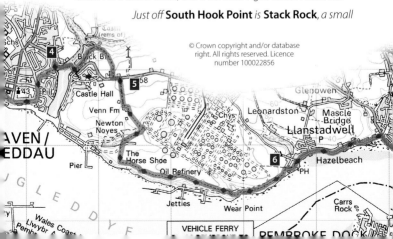

Messing about: *Ocean-going yachts crowd Milford Haven Marina*

island that is home to another fort from the mid-nineteenth century. In total, 12 forts were built in the Milford Haven area during the 1850s and 1860s to protect this important deep-water channel from attack by the French. They are known as Palmerston forts because of their close connection with the Prime Minister at the time, Lord Palmerston.

Strategically significant back in Victorian times, Milford Haven remains an important waterway today. Over the next couple of days, you will undoubtedly see huge oil tankers making their way up and down this channel. As well as being the UK's third largest port, the Haven is one of the deepest natural waterways in the world. It was formed when a river valley was flooded as sea levels rose at the end of the last glacial period. Its depth means it is able to handle some of the largest ocean-going vessels. The area's first oil terminal and oil refinery was opened in 1960 and, today, Milford Haven handles almost one-third of Britain's seaborne trade in oil and gas.

The oil industry sites gradually make their presence felt as you make your way south-east from **Sandy Haven**: subtly at first, in the form of a quiet background hum coming from somewhere up to your left. Then you'll see the wire fence, then some storage tanks and then the high-tech jetties

used to carry the liquefied natural gas (LNG) via pipeline from ships to the terminal to be re-gassified. The path passes under the first jetty on a soft, sandy beach. The next section of path is surfaced. This gradually drops you into **Gelliswick Bay**.

2 Continue past the **sailing club** and round to the left. Part-way up the hill, climb the steps on the right. The path brings you out next to **Hakin Infants School**, on the edge of a residential area. Follow the road, **Picton Road**,

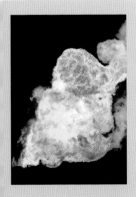

Raging inferno

Pembroke Dock was established in 1814 when the Royal Navy Dockyard was set up. Before it closed in 1926, workers had built five royal yachts and 263 other vessels. From 1930 until 1957, Pembroke Dock served as an RAF base and, during World War Two, huge hangars housed the Sunderland flying boats. The dock inevitably attracted the interest of the Luftwaffe, and was heavily bombed. One raid resulted in an oil tank fire that raged for 18 days.

Heading upriver: *Yachts in a chandler's yard at Hazelbeach*

round to the right, soon heading downhill. At a staggered crossroads with a convenience store on the corner, go straight across.

3 Having reached a T-junction close to a Tesco store — with the library and **Tourist Information Centre** nearby — turn right to cross the **fly-over** and then go right again at the roundabout — along **Victoria Road**. You soon climb up into **Milford Haven**. With a **new marina** down to the right and attractive Georgian terraces up to the left, this is a good-looking part of town.

You will pass the **war memorial** and then, with a red obelisk in the middle of the junction, you'll see two roads to the right. Take the second (higher) of these, known as **The Rath**. The gardens on the southern side contain a **statue of a fisherman** gathering his nets. The inscription below reads: 'Thanks to them, Milford Haven flourished.'

The town of Milford Haven was established in 1793 by Sir William Hamilton, the cuckolded husband of Nelson's mistress Emma Hamilton. Originally centred around a whaling fleet and some shipbuilding, the town later became a commercial port with a large and successful fishing industry — hence the statue on The Rath.

Turning your back on the water, follow the road round to the left. Soon after passing a pub and convenience store, turn right down **Pill Green**, which becomes **Cellar Hill**. A few metres beyond the social club, take the waymarked path through the trees on the left. This leads to a **slipway**, along which you turn left.

4 Go right at the road, keeping a wary eye and ear on the traffic, particularly on the bends. **Castle Pill** is crossed via **Black Bridge**, after which you turn left along a surfaced track in front of **Blackbridge Cottage**. Take the path heading up into the trees on the right. This quickly re-crosses the surfaced lane and continues along the top of an **embankment**. You later emerge close to the water's edge again. The path joins a track, soon after which you need to take the muddy track on the right and then bear left. As the track reaches a gate, take the narrower path on the left — effectively continuing in the same direction. Bear right along a vehicle track.

5 Turn left along the busy road (there is no pavement) and then take the track on the right — towards **Venn Farm**. At the farmyard entrance, bear right. When this track ends, go through the gate over to the left and then cross the field to a small gate in the fence opposite. Once through this, drop to another gate, followed by a bridge in the woods. The path gradually weaves its way back to the shore, crossing one dirt track on the way.

Three **metal bridges** are used to cross two groups of pipelines and an access road servicing the second gas terminal of the day. The last of these is followed by a woodland path that forms a refreshing antidote to the industrial trappings of the last few hundred metres.

Nearing buildings on the edge of **Hazelbeach**, there is a clear view across to Pembroke Dock on the other side of the waterway. The Cleddau Bridge is also visible.

6 Bear right after a metal kissing-gate and drop to a surfaced lane. Passing some large houses along the way, drop to a T-junction close to the **Ferry House Inn**. Turn right, keeping to the shore road through **Llanstadwell**. Turn right at the next T-junction — along **Trafalgar Terrace**, heading into **Neyland**.

You'll be pleased to discover that tankers don't come this far upstream; you are more likely to see yachts, motorboats and the odd jet-skier in the waters around Neyland and Pembroke Dock. Indeed, further along the road, you will pass **Neyland Yacht Club**. The road starts swinging left after this.

Up until 1856, Neyland was just a small fishing village, but, having rejected Aber Mawr on the north coast, the Victorian engineer Isambard Kingdom Brunel decided to make this the western terminus of his South Wales Railway. Port facilities were also built and, for many years, Neyland handled the busy packet service across the Irish Sea, although grand plans for trans-Atlantic trade never materialised. Sadly, when the railway was axed in 1965, the ferry service followed soon after and Neyland's heyday was over.

7 Having climbed away from the shore, turn right along **Cambrian Road**. After several hundred metres, watch for a fingerpost directing you towards Pembroke Dock — down through the trees on the right. This winding woodland trail provides the link between Neyland and the busy A477. Turn right when you reach the main road. There is a walkway beside it, which is just as well because you have to endure it for the next 2 kilometres. The road crosses high above **Westfield Pill,** giving you a bird's eye view of the marina below. The next bridge is the mighty 👁 **Cleddau Bridge**, which opened in 1975, replacing a ferry service that had operated since 1858. Finally, you have crossed to the southern side of the **Milford Haven** waterway. Pass beside the toll booths — there is no charge for pedestrians.

A 19th-century cannon overlooks Milford Haven waterway close to the Cleddau Bridge

Airy crossing: *The Cleddau Bridge takes walkers to the far side of the Milford Haven waterway*

8 Turn right at the roundabout and then take the road on the left — **Essex Road**. Follow this round to the left and downhill, keeping left at a mini-roundabout. This is now **Tremeyrick Street**. Follow it to its junction with one of 👁 **Pembroke Dock's** main roads, the **A4139**.

From the bottom of Tremeyrick Street, you need to aim for the Asda petrol station over to the right. This is a complicated junction, but the easiest way to get there is to turn right and then, with the Travelodge behind you, cross the road and head down the next road on the right — **Western Way**. You'll pass the petrol station on your right and the Asda supermarket on your left. Just after the supermarket, turn right along **Front Street**, which has a nineteenth-century gun tower at the end of it.

Follow the road round to the left and then turn right along **Pembroke Street**. Follow this uphill, going straight over at a couple of junctions.

9 When the road bends left, cross over and join a path rising through the trees to the right. Keep straight on until reaching an asphalt path, along which you turn left. This comes out on to a quiet road, **Presely View**, next to the **Defensible Barracks**, another military site dating from the 1850s, now in a bad state of disrepair. Follow this road round to the right and then the left to drop to a T-junction with **Treowen Road**.

Turn right. At a dip in the road, take the surfaced path on the left — through a small patch of woodland. Emerging on to **Sycamore Street**, bear right. At the bottom, go through a gate to access a rough track which crosses an open area. Just in front of the next gate and stile, head up the muddy path on the left. At the top of the rise, go through the metal kissing-gate and keep straight ahead. Keep close to the field boundary on your right until you reach a small stream in a wooded dip. Cross this and head up the waymarked path opposite.

Emerging from the trees, there is no path on the ground, but walkers should head straight across the field to a stile beside a gate, partly hidden by trees. Cross this and go through the gate opposite to continue across the next field in roughly the same direction. After a gate in the bottom corner, another small stream is crossed via **stepping stones**. A trail heads right and up through the trees, emerging on a wider path close to the mud banks beside the **Pembroke River.** Drop to the right.

Approaching **Pembroke**, you catch your first glimpse of the substantial and impressive remains of its Norman castle across the rooftops to your right. Turn right on reaching the road and then, as this swings left, take the surfaced path dropping down to the edge of the town's **Mill Pond**, directly opposite 👁 **Pembroke Castle**. Turn left to reach the northern side of the road bridge, known as **Mill Bridge.**

The waterside buildings here used to be warehouses. They would have stored the lime, coal, agricultural produce and even French wine that once passed through the sheltered harbour at **Pembroke***.*

Pembroke Castle was the birthplace of Henry VII

Like many Landsker churches, St James' at Manorbier features a tall defensive tower

Landsker line

Little England beyond Wales

As you walk from the northern end to the southern end of the Pembrokeshire Coast Path, you'll notice changes: in the place names on maps, in historical references and even in the language local people speak. While north Pembrokeshire is a Welsh-speaking area, the south isn't; and the line dividing the two is known as the Landsker Line.

The Celtic language that evolved into Welsh is thought to have arrived in Britain in about 600BC. This largely survived the Roman invasion, but didn't fare so well against the Norman invaders or, more significantly, their English followers...

The Normans and their supporters were building castles in south Pembrokeshire, such as those at Pembroke and Manorbier, by the end of the eleventh century. The invaders were not interested in the relatively inhospitable, less fertile lands in the north of the county, so the Welsh speakers there got on with their lives with little interference.

Of course, the language has had its ups and down since then. Henry VIII's 1536 Act of Union, for instance, banned Welsh-only speakers from public office. At the other end of the scale, the eighteenth century saw a revival as the intelligentsia developed an interest in Celtic history.

More information: A Welsh Government document outlines the history of the language. It can be downloaded from www.wales.gov.uk

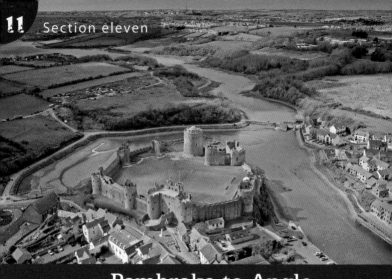

Pembroke to Angle

Distance: *18 kilometres / 11 miles* | **Start:** *Northern side of Mill Bridge, Pembroke SM 983 016* | **Finish:** *Eastern edge of Angle village SM 866 028* | **Maps:** *Ordnance Survey Explorer OL36 South Pembrokeshire, Landranger 157 St Davids & Haverfordwest*

Outline: The second full day on the Milford Haven waterway sees walkers turning their backs on the towns and heading out into the countryside.
This section starts close to the stunning ruins of medieval Pembroke Castle, the birthplace in the fifteenth century of Henry VII. Secret patches of woodland and farm paths then lead towards the power station and oil refinery. These are not the most attractive of constructions, but they remain hidden from view for much of the time and are surrounded by pretty countryside. Finally turning your back on Milford Haven's industry, you head out beside the water to the attractive village of Angle.

Services: *Pembroke has plenty of accommodation, places to eat, shops, public toilets and banks with cash machines. (Pembroke TIC | 01437 776499 | pembroke.tic@pembrokeshire.gov.uk.) There's a small convenience store in Monkton, but, after that, there are no facilities until Angle, where there are a couple of pubs, a campsite, a small shop with cash machine (fee payable) and public toilets. Castle Cars, Pembroke | 01646 622440*

Don't miss: Wogan's Cavern – natural cave in wall of Pembroke Castle | **Monkton** – priory remains and associated buildings | **Fort Popton** – a Palmerston fort built in the nineteenth century

▲ *Pembroke Castle from the air*

Pembroke/Penfro

The lovely town of Pembroke comes as a refreshing surprise after the slightly run-down feel of its neighbour, Pembroke Dock. With the sturdy curtain walls and mighty keep of its Norman castle dominating, this small town on the Pembroke River is steeped in history. At one point, it controlled all local trade as all goods entering the Milford Haven waterway had to be landed here. An important stronghold for the Anglo-Normans, it also became important in the control of 'Little England' in the Middle Ages, and, significantly, never fell to the Welsh.

One of the most dramatic events in the town's history was the siege of 1648, during the English Civil War. The Parliamentarian commander of the castle, Colonel John Poyer, suddenly switched allegiance, incurring the wrath of Oliver Cromwell. Cromwell himself led the attack on Pembroke Castle, and the ensuing siege lasted 48 days, ending only when Parliamentarian forces cut off the defenders' water supply. Poyer and the other two rebellion leaders were condemned to death, although the State Council, in a moment of leniency, decided that only one should be executed. In a decision taken by casting lots, Poyer drew the short straw.

Looking down on the river from the top of Pembroke Castle

The route: **Pembroke to Angle**

1 From the northern side of **Mill Bridge** in **Pembroke**, turn right to cross the road bridge and immediately go right again to enter South Quay car park. Here you pick up a path around the base of **Pembroke Castle**'s tremendous walls with the **Mill Pond** on your right. There are plenty of benches along this path, a chance to sit and soak up the fine atmosphere of this historic location.

As you walk your partial circuit of this impressive structure, watch for the iron grille leading into 👁 **Wogan's Cavern**, a natural limestone cavern over which the castle was built. *It is thought the castle inhabitants used it as a storehouse and possibly a boathouse. There used to be a ditch running from the cave down to the river.*

Turn right at the road. When it narrows, go up the lane on your right, between stone walls, soon passing 👁 **Monkton Old Hall**, the **church** and **priory remains**.

Turning right along the main road through **Monkton**, you'll soon pass your final shop until Angle, so make sure you've got enough supplies to last you to the end of the day.

Leaving Monkton behind, the road bends sharp left. As it does so, take the narrow road on the right. This drops past **Quoits Mill** — once the site of an old water mill — and swings round the side of **Quoits Water Pill**. As the lane bends away from the mud banks, you pass **Fleet Cottage**. A few metres beyond this, take the waymarked path through the trees on your right. Keep close to the field boundary on your right after the gate.

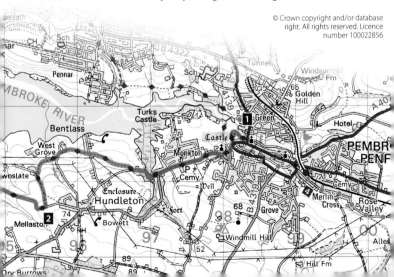

Wogan's Cavern: *Pembroke Castle is built over a natural limestone cave once used as a storeroom*

As you cross a rough track, you'll see the power station and oil refinery ahead. A sewage works access road leads down to a lane. Cross over and climb the stile next to the gate opposite. Keep close to the fence on your right and you will drop to a wooden stile, after which a small stream is crossed.

A shady path brings you out near **West Grove Barns**. Follow the broad track and then take the overgrown path on your left. Turn left along the surfaced track and, almost immediately, go up the steps to the right. Walk with the fence on your left and then go through two gates in quick succession.

The path now passes along a shady ditch before heading up the field beside the fence on the right. Watch carefully for a stile in this fence. This provides access to a trail that drops and awkwardly crosses **two streams** in quick succession. Immediately climb the steep, grassy embankment on your left — close to the buildings of **Brownslate** — and turn left along the surfaced farm lane.

2 Turn right at the road and walk along the asphalt for about 1.2 kilometres.

*The true extent of the industrial complexes of **Milford Haven** becomes apparent now. Ahead are the buildings and chimneys of the oil refinery and power station that will become dominant features on today's walk; on the other side of the water are the enormous storage tanks of the LNG terminals passed yesterday.*

Supersize: *An oil tanker alongside one of the high-tech Milford Haven jetties*

After passing **Whim Cottage**, the road drops into a dip. Just before it starts climbing again, go through a small gate set back slightly from the road on your right. This potentially muddy path follows a stream for a short while, towards **Goldborough Pill**, and then forks just after a gate. Bear left here, and then go through a small wooden gate at the top of the rise.

The path ahead is reasonably clear now as it goes through another two gates and climbs beside a wire fence. It then goes through another gate and drops steeply through **bluebell woods** to a path junction. Turn left here and then bear right at a waymarked fork, quickly going through a gate and then climbing beyond the stream.

3 On reaching **Lambeeth Farm**, turn left and then right. Keep straight ahead: through a small gate and then through a large metal gate to pass to the left of a single-storey, white building. Keep to the left side of the next field.

Keep straight ahead after the next small gate, following an obvious line between banks of high hedges and trees. The power station is down to your right, but it is hidden from view much of the time — except where the route crosses tracks or open areas. A little further on, as the path widens, it is the chimneys and flares of the oil refinery that dominate the scene.

There has been a power station on the south bank of the Pembroke River, close to Pennar Mouth, since 1968. The first one was oil-fired, but that closed in 1999. In 2012, a combined cycle gas turbine plant opened, with the potential to generate enough power for 3.5 million homes. According to owners RWE npower, the state-of-the-art technology makes Pembroke one of the most efficient power stations of its kind in Europe.

Hospitable monks

Towards the end of the eleventh century, Benedictine monks established a priory at Monkton. All that remains today are some arches, the Priory Farmhouse and Old Monkton Hall. Hospitality was a key requirement of Benedictine rule, so many monasteries played the role of inn. Although Monkton was only small, it was close to a powerful castle and on the pilgrims' route to St Davids, so it would probably have seen a fair number of travellers.

4 Cross the power station's access road diagonally left to pick up a path through the trees. Turn left along a quiet lane and then right at a T-junction. This lane swings right as it passes the church at **Pwllcrochan**.

The church building and its graveyard are used as an educational nature centre by local schools. Not long ago though, it served a small but thriving community, many of whom farmed the oyster and cockle beds of the nearby Pwllcrochan Flats. Families began to drift away from Pwllcrochan and nearby Rhoscrowther after the oil refinery was built in 1964. Many more left after a large explosion at the site in 1994. Twenty-six people were hurt in the blast, which damaged homes within a 16-kilometre radius and was heard up to 60 kilometres away. It took 130 firefighters from as far afield as Cardiff and Swansea several hours to extinguish the resulting blaze. Many residents of Rhoscrowther then leapt at the offer, made by Texaco two years earlier, to purchase their homes. Most of those properties have since been demolished.

Beyond a bridge, the lane becomes a rough track and begins climbing. You are soon walking beside the razor wire-topped fence of the **oil refinery.**

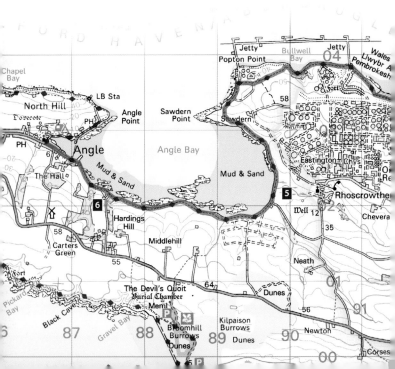

Keep close to the fence after a stile and then swing left along a faint trail as the fence performs a sharp turn to the left. Watch carefully for a fingerpost which directs walkers down the slope — in the general direction of the **jetty** below. The way isn't clear at first, but you then pick up an obvious path that drops close to the water's edge. Walk under the pipelines and then climb the narrow path on the other side.

A **lime kiln** and some ruins are passed above a small sandy beach at **Bulwell Bay**. Soon after this, the path begins heading inland. It comes out on to a surfaced area near **Fort Popton**, from where you can look across Angle Bay to Angle.

👁 **Fort Popton** *is another of the Palmerston forts built to protect Milford Haven from attack by the French. It served another defensive function in World War Two when the RAF moved in. Today, it is owned by Valero, the company that has run the oil refinery since 2011.*

Go straight across at a series of road junctions to head downhill, past a 20mph speed limit sign and keeping right at the next junction. Turn left at a T-junction at the bottom of the slope. This road skirts the edge of **Angle Bay**, often with clear views of the oil refinery. Rather strangely, something about this sight always puts me in mind of the skyline of the city of Oz in The Wizard of Oz!

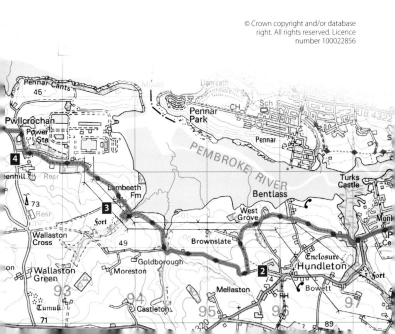

Gerald of Wales was Bishop elect at Saint Davids Cathedral

Gerald of Wales

Famous chronicler of medieval Wales

Pick up any book on the history of Wales, and it's likely that you will come across a reference to Gerald of Wales. Born in Manorbier Castle in 1146 (see page 195), he became a senior clergyman, scholar, traveller and writer. His pedigree was impeccable: his mother, Angharad FitzGerald, a Welsh princess; and his father, William FitzOdo de Barri, one of Wales' most powerful knights.

He wrote books on Ireland, but it is his books on Wales for which he is best known. The *Itinerarium Cambriae* (Journey Through Wales) and *Descriptio Cambriae* (Description of Wales) remain important today as sources of historical information about life in medieval Wales. They describe places visited and sights seen during a tour of the country in 1188 — ostensibly to enlist men for the Third Crusade.

He served four years as Bishop elect at Wales' most important cathedral, but neither the king nor the archbishop of Canterbury would ever allow him to become Bishop there — largely because his Welsh ancestry was seen as a threat. He even tried to persuade the Pope that St David's Cathedral should have the same status as Canterbury.

More information: The manuscripts of several of Gerald's books, including the *Itinerarium Cambriae*, are now kept at the British Library. Digitised versions can be viewed online at www.bl.uk.

Glorious mud: *Angle Bay's mudflats provide superb habitat for waders and wildfowl*

5 On reaching a fenced compound, pass between the concrete blocks on your right to walk beside the **beach**. The path eventually climbs a little, but at no point can it justifiably be called a 'cliff path'. Keep to the far edge of the fields as you wend your way west, bidding a final, far-from-tearful farewell to the oil industry.

The sheltered bay to the right is **Angle Bay**. *This contains a wide range of habitats and its mudflats are an important winter feeding ground for a number of bird species, including waders and wigeon, which migrate annually from Scandinavia and Siberia.*

6 The path eventually enters woods and reaches a track. Without going down on to the beach itself, bear right here. On reaching the next track — surfaced this time — bear right again. After a large gate, continue up the lane. On the edge of **Angle village**, you'll pass and ignore a road to Pembroke on the left. About 150 metres after this, you'll see a small white building on the right with several signs on it, including one to the lifeboat station and another for The Old Point House. Tomorrow's path goes along the track on the right here, but those intent on spending the night in the village should continue along the road for a few more metres yet.

Angle to St Govan's Chapel

Distance: *27 kilometres / 17 miles* | **Start:** *Eastern edge of Angle village SM 866 028*
Finish: *St Govan's Chapel, 1.8 km south of Bosherston SR 966 930* | **Maps:** *Ordnance Survey Explorer OL36 South Pembrokeshire, Landranger 157 St Davids & Haverfordwest and 158 Tenby and Pembroke*

Outline: Leaving the Milford Haven waterway, this section heads back on to the cliffs and ends amid some truly spectacular limestone scenery. Leaving Angle, the path heads round to the southern side of the Angle peninsula for the first view of the open sea in days. And what a view! The route heads east along the undulating cliffs and then crosses the beautiful beach at Freshwater West before being forced inland by the MoD's Castlemartin range. If there is no firing taking place, it later drops back to the coast for a spectacular section of limestone cliffs that ends at a fantastically placed chapel. If the range is in use, the inland detour is via lanes and farm paths.

Services: *Angle has a couple of pubs, a campsite and a small shop with cash machine (fee payable). (Pembroke TIC | 01437 776499 | pembroke.tic@pembrokeshire. gov.uk.) There are B&Bs in Merrion on the 'live-firing alternative' route; otherwise, the only accommodation and food is in Bosherston, 1.8km north of St Govan's Chapel. Public toilets in Angle, West Angle Bay, Freshwater West and Bosherston. Castle Cars, Pembroke | 01646 622440*

👁 **Don't miss:** Angle – fifteenth-century fishermen's chapel | **Green Bridge of Wales** – spectacular natural sea arch | **Huntsman's Leap** – impressive, narrow chasm cutting into cliffs

▲ *A rare 15th-century Welsh Tower House at Angle*

Angle

At first glance, there doesn't seem to be much to  **Angle**: just a couple of rows of cottages stretched out along either side of the road close to the end of Angle Peninsula. Take a leisurely stroll around this peaceful conservation village though and you'll discover a castle, possibly built as a defence against the Welsh forces of Owain Glyndŵr; a fifteenth-century fishermen's chapel in the grounds of St Mary's Church, where the bodies of unknown seamen would've been prepared for burial; and the rather grand building of the former Globe Hotel. And all surrounded by a medieval field system.

The lifeboat station, first opened in 1868 and moved to its current location in 1927, is the pride of the village. Over the years, many crew members have received medals for noteworthy rescues. One of the most famous of these took place in 1894 when the schooner, the *Loch Shiel,* struck the rocks on nearby Thorn Island. The Angle lifeboat was despatched and, although it was unable to reach the vessel, several crew members risked their lives by clambering on to the island and getting a rope to the ship. All on board were saved. (See page 177 for how the *Loch Shiel* wreck came to be known as Wales' 'Whisky Galore'.)

Looking across Angle Bay at high tide to the Old Point House pub

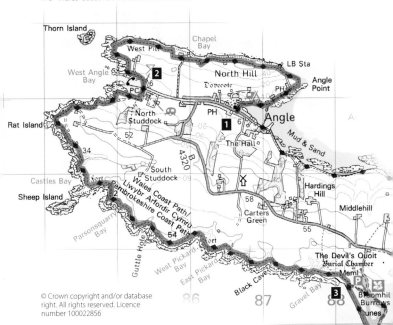

The route: **Angle to St Govan's Chapel**

1 From the small white building seen on the way into **Angle**
yesterday, take the track north towards **The Old Point House**.
Bear right after the bridge and follow the track around the edge
of the lovely bay until it ends at the pub, which dates back to at
least the sixteenth century. (This track may briefly become flooded
during some high tides.) Keep right as you cross the parking area and
you'll find a gate leading on to a grassy path. After rounding **Angle Point,**
cross the lifeboat station track.

The path winds its way along the edge of fields and through woods,
joining a track close to the charmingly isolated cottages of **Chapel Bay**.
When this swings left close to **Chapel Bay Fort**, go through the small gate
opposite to resume walking on the mostly grassy path.

Chapel Bay Fort was constructed in 1891 and is thought to be one of the ear-
liest examples of a fort built from concrete with no reinforcement. Surrounded
by a 10 metre-deep dry moat, it contains barracks for 100 men, which formed
part of the defences of Milford Haven waterway during World War One. It is now
open to the public.

Red fort: *Sunset colours the 'Palmerston fort' on Thorn Island*

From the low cliffs around **West Angle Bay** — and yes! these are cliffs now! — you can see across to St Ann's Head, visited on Day Section nine of the route, but just 4.3 kilometres away as the crow flies.

Closer in to the shore is **Thorn Island**, home to yet another Palmerston fort — one that, for a few years, served as an hotel.

It was on the rocks of Thorn Island that the Loch Shiel *met her fate on January 30, 1894. Bound for Australia, she'd been carrying a cargo of whisky and gunpowder, and, after local lifeboat men had bravely rescued her crew and passengers, the second part of the story of the shipwreck began to unfold... As the*

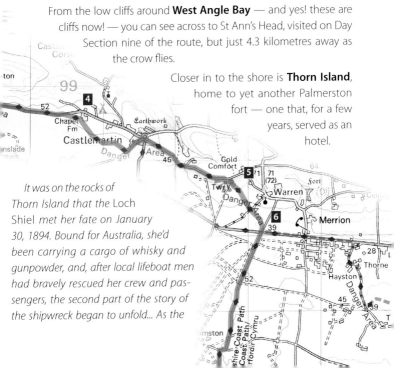

Historic ruin: *East Blockhouse was built by the Tudors to protect Milford Haven against the Spanish*

schooner began to break up, her cargo was washed up in local bays and on the peninsula's beaches. Soon learning of the contents of some of the cases, local people ran down to the sea to salvage what they could from the waves. Customs men tried to retrieve the looted goods, but managed to recover only a portion of what had come ashore. It is said they apprehended a number of local people who were carrying home cases of gunpowder in the mistaken belief they'd found whisky.

2 Coming in to West Angle Bay, ignore any paths to the right. A broad track drops you close to the car park. Keep to the right of the low wall beside the beach. The onward coast path goes through a gate to the left of the toilet block.

West Angle Bay contains a pretty, sheltered beach with plenty of interesting rock pools that always prove popular with visiting families and school groups. It is designated as a Site of Special Scientific Interest and, in 1979, a previously unknown species of cushion starfish was discovered here: Asterina phylactica. *Unfortunately, numbers of this rare echinoderm fell dramatically after the* Sea Empress *oil spill of 1996.*

Usual clifftop rules apply at this point: keep right at most forks unless the path is obviously heading down the cliff. The latter becomes more relevant later — on the southern side of the peninsula — where some paths totter worryingly close to the cliff edge and sheep trods really do just drop off into oblivion.

Overlooking **Rat Island** *is* **East Blockhouse,** *the remains of a defensive structure built during Tudor times to protect Milford Haven from attack by the Spanish. West Blockhouse, the site of its twin near St Ann's Head, was passed during Day Section nine, although nothing remains of this structure.*

A treat awaits after passing the ruins of East Blockhouse — the open sea. It's the first time in days that walkers on the National Trail have been able to look out at the distant blue horizon. This is what coastal walking is all about! Although the tops of the oil refinery stacks can be seen from time to time, it's the sea stacks in the waters below that now catch the attention — those and the natural arches, the islands, the dramatic cliffs...

Soon after passing **Sheep Island**, you come to a farm gate. Cross the stile on the right. After passing a small building, watch for the impressive arch in the cliffs below, **Guttle Hole**. The beautiful golden sweep of beaches formed by Freshwater West and Frainslake Sands soon appear, backed by high dunes. (The latter is on MoD land and, sadly, has no public access.)

The path dips, not once but twice, and on steep, loose ground around the boulder-strewn bay of **West Pickard Bay**. The path then continues in an undulating manner all the way to **Freshwater West**. It's a great stretch of coast, but hard work!

Freshwater West is one of Pembrokeshire's finest beaches, although strong rip currents make it unsuitable for swimmers. It is, however, very popular with experienced surfers and annually hosts the Welsh National Surfing Championships.

Thatched seaweed-drying hut at Freshwater West

Wave power: *The setting sun catches the spectacular twin limestone pillars of Stack Rocks*

This impressive beach has been used as a location in recent films. Ridley Scott's 2010 Robin Hood, starring Russell Crowe and Cate Blanchett, used it for a battle scene. Other nearby locations in the same film included Angle and Pembroke Dock. Scenes involving Dobby the house-elf in both parts of the Harry Potter and the Deathly Hallows films were also shot here.

The tiny, thatched hut on the foreshore, recently rebuilt, would once have been used to dry Porphyra umbilicalis, *a type of edible seaweed used to make the Welsh delicacy laverbread. Give it a try while you're walking the coast: like Marmite you'll either love it or hate it.*

3 As soon as you reach the dunes at the back of the beach at Freshwater West, you have a choice, depending on what the tide is doing: you can either drop to the beach and walk to its southern end where a path leads up to the road and main car park (with toilet block). Or:

> **High tide alternative**: *Inland loop, avoiding the shore*
> Continue on a path through the sand and grass to the road and then turn right to reach the main car park in about 700 metres.

From the main car park, the **official route** continues southeast along the

road, soon walking beside the Army's **Castlemartin Firing Range**. If the red flags are flying, it means the range is in use and you will not be able to use the path along the cliffs from **Stack Rocks,** marked on some maps as **Elegug Stacks**. (The alternative, detailed later, uses quiet lanes and farm paths, a considerable improvement on the old route, which was practically all on roads.)

About 1 kilometre beyond the main beach car park at Freshwater West,

Elegug Stacks

Stack Rocks, or Elegug Stacks, consists of a pair of limestone towers, standing detached from the cliffs. Elegug is the local name for the guillemot, and you've a good chance of spotting large colonies of these black and white birds — as well as razorbills, cormorants, kittiwakes and fulmars — along this stretch of the coast during spring and summer. You may even be lucky enough to spot choughs and peregrines.

you will see a panel on your right with information about the **Castlemartin Range Trail.** This permissive path enables you to get off the road and, later on, it provides an alternative route across farmland when the cliff path from Stack Rocks is shut. You can join it at this panel. At first, it simply runs along the broad grass verge, but then, after passing a sentry post, it goes through a small metal gate to use a fenced strip of ground — a sort of no man's land between the road on your left and the range on your right. The permissive trail runs parallel with the road until you near **Chapel Farm**.

4 As you pass to the right of the buildings at **Chapel Farm**, turn right through the small metal gate. A series of these gates, with the green Castlemartin Range Trail waymarkers on them, guides you across a couple of fields. Crossing a rough track, you enter a large field where you should keep close to the fence on the left. After the next gate, aim for the small building ahead and turn left along the track.

At the small roundabout, take the road for 'Warren' and 'St Twynnells'. Almost immediately, go through the small gate on the right and walk along the field edge. Walk parallel with the road — until reaching the **control tower.**

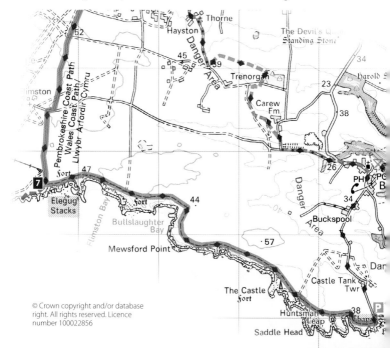

Rock of ages: *The 'Green Bridge of Wales' is one of the finest natural sea arches in Britain*

Lying on a ridge of high ground a few kilometres back from the coast, this tower is used to control tank movements on the range to the south. Members of the public often park up nearby to watch the manoeuvres from a safe distance.

The area to the south consists of flat, limestone grassland — a plateau that suddenly ends at the dramatic cliff edge. The Carboniferous limestone here was formed about 350 million years ago. The plateau itself would've been created by marine erosion when the sea level was higher than it is today. Movements in the Earth's crust about 50 million years ago would then have lifted it roughly into its present position.

5 Here, the path goes right and then left to pass to the right of the tower. After the next small gate, pass around the top end of a line of gorse bushes and then swing half-right to a gap in the hedge. Continue in the same direction down to a gate. Swing right, through a gate, over a track and then straight across the field to reach the road. Turn right along the asphalt.

6 At a crossroads, if the range is not in use, walkers can go straight across and follow the road to where it ends, close to **Stack Rocks**. (If firing is taking place, see 'live-firing alternative' route below.)

7 The coastal path goes off to the left at the road-end.

Sunless slit: *The dramatic natural cleft called Huntman's Leap*

Detour: *To a spectacular natural sea arch*

To visit the remarkable 👁 **Green Bridge of Wales**, turn right, on the signposted path. A visit is highly recommended before you continue east. *On a wild day, with the waves crashing up against the rocks, and with the stacks just off to the east, this is a truly awesome place to stand and contemplate the power of the mighty sea.*

Continuing on the **official route**, you soon pass through a small gate to find yourself on a broad track that keeps some metres back from the cliff edge. If you stick with this, you will miss some of the most fascinating coastal scenery in the whole of Pembrokeshire: stacks, natural arches, zawns, blow-holes... However, if you decide to use the narrower trails along the edge of the cliffs, you need to take extra care, always mindful of the weather and ground conditions as well as the fact that this is a military range. Do not touch any metal objects!

The small headland on the western side of **Flimston Bay** has ancient embankments and ditches across its neck, indicating that Iron Age people once occupied it. This tiny peninsula is riddled with caves, and, at its far end, is one of the most impressive blowholes in the area: **The Cauldron.**

Further east along the coast are more blowholes, more stacks and more caves. Some of the latter have been found to contain traces of Stone Age habitation.

Folding in the Carboniferous limestone between Flimston Bay and **Mewsford Point** *was caused by continents colliding about 290 million years ago.*

Finally, 5 kilometres after leaving Stack Rocks — and just beyond the amazing narrow chasm of 👁 **Huntsman's Leap** — you reach the sentry box on the edge of this part of the range. Go through the gate to reach the road-end close to **St Govan's Chapel**. To visit the spectacularly located chapel, take the trail on the right; those spending the night in **Bosherston**, which is 1.8 kilometres to the north, should turn left along the road.

Live-firing alternative: *Avoiding the army testing range*

If live firing is taking place, turn left at the crossroads and then go through a small gate on the right to access the permissive path again. Keep close to the fence on your left. After an uncultivated strip, you come out on the road in front of **Merrion Camp**. Continue along the road. About 350 metres after passing the display tanks at the camp's entrance, take the lane on the right — signposted 'Thorne Chapel'. This eventually ends at a junction with a broad track on the edge of the range. Turn left and immediately go through the gate on the left. Walking through long grass, keep close to the fence on the left, eventually following it up to the right to come back out on to the concrete track. Go through the small gate opposite and bear right, crossing to the fence corner. Turn left with the fence and then left again after the next gate. Stay with the fence through another two gates and then swing left to leave the range. Turn right along the track and go left at the bottom. Coming out on to the road, turn right to enter Bosherston. If you wish to reach St Govan's Chapel, follow the road round to the right after the church.

High limestone cliffs dominate St Govan's Head

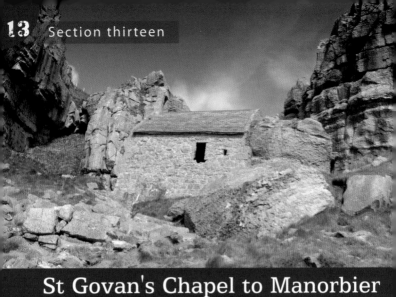

St Govan's Chapel to Manorbier

Distance: *17 kilometres / 11 miles* | **Start:** *St Govan's Chapel, 1.8km south of Bosherston SR 966 930* | **Finish:** *Manorbier Bay SS 060 976* | **Maps:** *Ordnance Survey Explorer OL36 South Pembrokeshire, Landranger 158 Tenby and Pembroke*

Outline: A varied day, starting on close-cropped turf atop limestone scenery, past gorgeous beaches, and ending with a roller-coaster cliff walk. The penultimate day begins with sublime walking on limestone cliffs. Even if you start from Bosherston, you'll be up on the cliffs soon after passing the delightful Lily Ponds. Stackpole Quay, preceded by beautiful Barafundle Bay and home to an excellent National Trust-run café, then marks the transition from limestone to red sandstone. The next cliff section is more strenuous, although several beaches provide tempting opportunities to stop and rest: the busy Freshwater East, secluded Swanlake Bay and, finally, Manorbier Bay.

Services: *B&Bs, pub, café and toilets in Bosherston, 1.8km north of St Govan's Chapel. Toilets at Broad Haven beach. Café and toilets at Stackpole Quay. Freshwater East has toilets, a campsite and an off-route pub. At the end of the section, Manorbier has accommodation, places to eat, a shop with cash machine (fee payable) and toilets. (Tenby TIC | 01834 842402 | tenby.tic@pembrokeshire.gov.uk.) Tenby Taxis | 01834 843678*

Don't miss: St Govan's Chapel – tiny, ancient church built into cliffs | **Bosherston Lily Ponds** – popular beauty spot and wildlife haven | **Stackpole Warren** – unusual limestone scenery including caves and blowholes

▲   *St Govan's Chapel is hidden in a rocky cove*

St Govan's Chapel

The diminutive St Govan's Chapel is one of the most iconic sights along the entire Pembrokeshire Coast Path. Built during the thirteenth century but restored in more recent times, it is tucked away in a cleft in the cliffs, hidden from sight until the walker descends a steep flight of steps. The rugged stairway leads directly into the chapel. Beyond is a tiny, rocky cove, endlessly pummelled by the sea. It's a wonderfully wild spot.

The chapel is thought to have been built on the site of a sixth-century hermit's retreat, the enigmatic St Govan. His, or her, identity has been lost in the mists of time; various suggestions include one of King Arthur's knights, the wife of a Glamorgan king or, most popularly, an Irish monk called Gobhan. Legend has it that Gobhan landed here after fleeing pirates from Lundy Island. A cleft is said to have opened up and concealed him until they had gone.

Stars swirl above St Govan's Chapel, concealed in its cleft in the cliffs

The route: **St Govan's Chapel to Manorbier**

1 From the road-end close to 👁 **St Govan's Chapel**, head east to resume your walk along the coast path. In about 300 metres — after passing some old **military bunkers** — take the gravel track on the left. (This bypasses St Govan's Head itself, but there is a public right-of-way that goes out on to the headland.) You'll leave the **Trevallen Downs** section of the **Castlemartin range** via a gate near a sentry box. The path is narrower now, but continue straight ahead — ignoring a couple of large gates up to the left — until you reach a small wooden gate.

Go through this and make your way towards the toilet block in the National Trust's **Broad Haven car park**. Then, just in front of the recycling bins, turn sharp right to drop to the gorgeous beach with its many hidden nooks and crannies — well worth exploring if you're not in a hurry. Pushing on along the coast path, keep close to the sand dunes, later swinging left to head inland slightly. Cross the small **bridge** at the back of the beach and then keep right. You'll quickly reach a fingerpost where you turn right along a sandy trail. This is where those who started the day in **Bosherston**, using the 'live-firing alternative' below, join the main route.

Sheltered sands: *Broad Haven beach and dunes with the distinctive Church Rock just offshore*

Live-firing alternative: *Avoiding the military range*
If the **Castlemartin range** is closed to the public, you'll need to start your day in **Bosherston**. Take the lane beside the church, signposted to the 'Lily Ponds'. Don't be tempted by the track; instead head into the National Trust car park, walk past the toilet block and then bear right at the fork. Drop to the first of the 👁 **Bosherston Lily Ponds** and turn left. Having crossed **two bridges**, go right at the T-junction. Turn right to cross a third, **smaller bridge**. Then, emerging from the trees, rejoin the main route at the next fingerpost where you turn left on to a sandy path.

2 Back on the **official route**, on reaching a fork, take either path to reach the top of the dunes overlooking **Broad Haven beach**. Take the path across the dunes and then drop to go through a gate.

The powers of nature have clearly been hard at work in the next bay round, creating some tremendous formations in the limestone cliffs. Watch for an impressive blowhole soon after the next gate. Some blowholes are the result of sea cave roofs collapsing; others are part of cave systems carved out by underground streams.

You can cut corners on the National Trust land at 👁 **Stackpole Warren**, but why would you want to do that on such a gorgeous, fascinating section of the coast? And the close-cropped grass makes for such easy walking across

Beautiful beach: *Barafundle Bay is protected by the National Trust*

the flat top that you'll almost inevitably want to linger. *As you do so, watch for razorbills, guillemots, fulmars and kittiwakes. Puffins and chough may also be seen, but they're less common.*

As on the Castlemartin Range further west, the cliffs along this stretch of the coast are extremely popular with climbers. **Mowingword** *and* **Stackpole Head** *itself are, in fact, generally regarded as world-class areas. Climbing restrictions are agreed on every year by the British Mountaineering Council and conservation bodies to ensure seabirds nesting on the cliffs are not disturbed.*

Sea-kayakers too love this stretch of coast and you'll often see them bobbing about in bays, threading through arches or just passing by, enjoying the scenery. A dark tunnel straight through the end of Stackpole Head offers an interesting shortcut for braver paddlers.

After coming in from **Stackpole Head**, the path goes through a gate and heads downhill. Just before you begin descending, go out to the right for a superb view of beautiful **Barafundle Bay** below, the winner of several 'best beach' accolades. Either cross the beach or the dunes and then climb the walled steps on the other side.

3 The next drop is to **Stackpole Quay** via a splendid, fairytale woodland. Go left at the path junction to drop to the toilets and tempting **National Trust café**.

Like the walled steps up from Barafundle Beach, the quay at Stackpole was built by the Cawdors in the eighteenth century. While limestone from the nearby quarry was shipped out, coal and luxury goods were brought in for Stackpole Court, the family's Palladian-style mansion. It was demolished in 1963.

Pond life

The short detour to the Bosherston Lily Ponds, passed on the live-firing alternative, is rewarded in June and July with a beautiful display of water lilies. The ponds are also home to dragonflies, damselflies, reed and sedge warblers, goosander, herons, otters and one of Britain's largest populations of greater horseshoe bats. They were created as part of a designed landscape in the eighteenth century by the Earls of Cawdor, who the Stackpole Estate.

Sand castle?: *Manorbier Castle sits on a mound at the back of the beach*

Climb the steps on the other side of the quay. One small, rocky bay is passed before you head back on to the cliffs. The flat-topped limestone cliffs are behind you now; ahead it's old red sandstone. It's a fairly long, steady climb to reach the highest point; and no sooner have you gone up, but the path drops again, albeit only slightly. And so it goes: a series of mild undulations, some less mild than others, as far as Freshwater East.

On the way, at **Greenala Point**, you'll pass another of the many **Iron Age forts** that are strung out all along the Pembrokeshire coast. Deep ditches and high embankments make up its formidable defences. Cross these to reach the tip of the peninsula for some good views back to Stackpole and ahead to Trewent Point: a suitable place to take stock as we approach the end of our epic journey.

4 Freshwater East is a tremendous arc of golden sand that is full of families on a sunny summer's day. Dropping to some buildings on the edge of the bay, ignore the track to the left; go straight across. This track passes some cottages and then swings left. As it does so, take a path on the right. This comes out close to the road and **public toilets**. Cross the bridge and then continue straight ahead, through a couple of gates, to head on to the dunes.

At dusk, in June and July, the dunes at Freshwater East are a good place to spot glow worms, a type of bioluminescent beetle. Its glowing abdomen performs two functions: as well as attracting a mate, it warns predators to stay away.

Keep to the main path through the dunes: the soft sand providing welcome relief for sore feet but creating extra work for tired muscles. Beyond the dunes, keep right at two forks, but ignore the path down to the beach. It's a fairly stiff climb back on to the cliffs, but that unbeatable feeling of being high above the waves, enjoying the breeze and looking out to the misty horizon — such a common sensation ever since leaving St Dogmael's — is ample reward. On a clear day, you may even be able to see the North Devon coast on the other side of the Bristol Channel.

5 The next beach, considerably smaller and quieter than the previous one, is at **Swanlake Bay.** Although not officially a naturists' beach, it is popular with nude bathers. The path then crosses an airy ridge over the top of **East Moor Cliff** before dropping on to a section of undercliff.

Go through a gate to pass to the right of some buildings and then follow the track up to the left. Take the next waymarked path on the right. This brings you out close to a parking area, at the far end of which, a path drops to the beach at **Manorbier**. Cross the first part of the beach and a small bridge.

Section 13 ends here, but the main part of Manorbier is about 700 metres northeast of the bay. To reach it, head up the path to the left after the bridge and then continue inland through the car park and past **Manorbier Castle**.

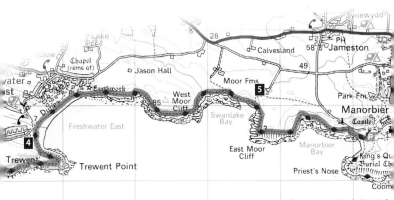

PEMBROKESHIRE COAST NATIONAL PARK/
PARC CENEDLAETHOL ARFORDIR PENFRO

Manorbier to Amroth Castle

Distance: *25 kilometres / 15 miles* | **Start:** *Manorbier Bay SS 060 976*
Finish: *Amroth Castle SN 171 072* | **Maps:** *Ordnance Survey Explorer OL36 South Pembrokeshire, Landranger 158 Tenby and Pembroke*

Outline: A day of great variety, including yet more breathtaking cliff scenery, sand dunes, a huge expanse of beach and woodland.

From Manorbier, the path takes to the cliffs again. If there's no firing at Penally, you get to walk the length of Tenby's fine South Beach. Take time out to explore the delightful town with its harbour, narrow lanes and old walls. The route then passes through attractive woods on a tough stretch between Tenby and Saundersfoot, and also makes use of a former mining railway, complete with tunnels. Sadly, no brass band awaits at Amroth Castle, journey's end, but there's a pub nearby for a celebratory drink.

Services: *Manorbier has accommodation, places to eat and a shop with cash machine. There are many places to stay and to eat all along this section, including Lydstep, Penally, Tenby, Saundersfoot, Wiseman's Bridge and Amroth. There are shops and banks with cash machines in Saundersfoot and Tenby, shops in Amroth and a launderette in Tenby. Toilets at Manorbier, Penally, Tenby, Saundersfoot, Wiseman's Bridge, Amroth and Amroth Castle. Pub at Amroth Castle. Tenby TIC | 01834 842402. National Park Visitor Centre at Tenby. Tenby Taxis | 01834 843678*

Don't miss: Manorbier Castle – fine Norman stronghold | **King's Quoit** – Neolithic burial chamber | **Tudor Merchant's House, Tenby** – fifteenth-century townhouse with Tudor-style furnishings

▲ *Tenby Old Town and harbour from the air*

Manorbier

The village of Manorbier is a pretty spot just up from the bay. The first thing walkers see as they approach the bay, whether from the west or the east, is the fine Norman  **Manorbier Castle**. The lands of Manorbier and Penally were granted to the knight Odo de Barri for his military assistance during the Norman conquest. His grandson, Gerald, was born in the castle in 1146 and went on to become the acclaimed clergyman, traveller and writer known as Gerald of Wales. In his 1188 book, *The Journey Through Wales*, he wrote: "In all the broad lands of Wales, Manorbier is the most pleasant place by far."

Today, the castle's impressive curtain walls still stand high and proud on the edge of high ground above the beach. Just outside the castle precincts are a recently restored dovecote and the ruins of an old watermill. Inside the walls, the Great Hall, several turrets and the chapel are among the many medieval buildings that remain. The castle is open to the public during the summer.

On the opposite side of the valley to the castle is the pretty twelfth-century church of St James with its fine, tall and slender tower.

Looking back towards Manorbier Castle from the King's Quoit

The route: **Manorbier to Amroth Castle**

1 Cross to the far, southeastern end of the beach at **Manorbier** where you'll find a set of steps hidden in a little recess. Climb these to regain the coastal route. The next section of splendid path doesn't climb particularly high: it cuts across the cliff face allowing you some excellent views of the rocks below.

You quickly pass 👁 **King's Quoit**, *a Neolithic burial chamber dating back to about 3,000BC. Flint microliths, used as the pointed tips of hunting weapons, have also been discovered in the Manorbier area — evidence of earlier, Mesolithic occupation.*

King's Quoit is soon followed by an incredibly **narrow cleft** through the rocks, one of several on this headland. Iron railings around the top of the chasm prevent walkers from tumbling into it. *The old red sandstone on this section of the coast is vertically faulted, enabling the sea to exploit weaknesses in it, creating fissures such as this one.* As you round the headland of **Priest's Nose** and look across to Old Castle Head, this vertical faulting is more clearly visible in the cliffs. Watch too for some impressive sea stacks near **Coomb**.

Beyond the attractive, sandy bay of **Presipe**, the coast path cuts across the neck of **Old Castle Head**, which is used by the Ministry of Defence as a missile firing range. Signs on gates have been warning for a while of the possibility of loud explosions and sudden flashes of light.

Coves, caves and arches: *Magnificent cliff scenery at Skrinkle Haven*

2 After a gate on the edge of the range — just above Presipe beach — keep straight ahead. Beyond the next gate, keep close to the perimeter fence. Follow this round to a road, along which you turn right. Take the next turning on the left, but then, staying with the fence for now, go through the gate on the right. (Those heading for **Skrinkle Haven youth hostel** should ignore this turning and keep to the road.) You part company with the fence at the next fingerpost: as the fence swings right, bear left.

After passing a parking area, you'll realise you're re-entering limestone country. There are some extremely impressive arches, caves and coves in the **Skrinkle Haven** area. Steep steps lead down into one of these coves, allowing a glimpse through the arches of **Church Doors**. If you choose to explore the coves, be aware that there is a very real danger of being cut off by the tide.

The path drops steeply at **Lydstep**. At the top of the next set of steps, the main route, peculiarly, goes left, missing out **Lydstep Point**.

Detour: *To Lydstep Point*
Turning right here, although not part of the official **Pembrokeshire Coast Path**, enables walkers to conduct a circuit of this delightful limestone headland and enjoy fabulous views from **Lydstep Point**. The slight diversion adds just 1.8 kilometres to the total distance.

Night sea: *The Milky Way arcs across the heavens above Caldey and St Margaret's islands*

3 If you decide to give Lydstep Point a miss and stay with the **official route**, having turned left at the top of the steps, you'll come out on to a track. Drop left and immediately turn right along a rough lane. This descends to **Lydstep Haven**, probably once a pleasant little cove before it was turned into a holiday park.

When the quarries on the northern side of Lydstep Point were operating in the nineteenth and early twentieth centuries, sailing vessels used to moor up beside a platform on the southern side of Lydstep Haven, loading limestone for delivery to ports in the Bristol Channel.

The lane bends left beside the beach. Take the gravel track on the right just after some benches and then drop to the beach. Continue to the far end, where you'll find some steps that lead back up on to the cliff. Keep right at an early fork, partly hidden by the thick bushes.

At one point, the path passes between the sea and a terrifying **chasm in the cliff** (it's a blowhole). Warning signs tell of the obvious dangers. Inland the scene is more benign, consisting of gently rolling farmland with fields divided by thick hedgerows and trees. Coming out over the top of **Proud**

Giltar, another limestone cliff that's popular with climbers, you can see **Caldey Island** and its neighbour **St Margaret's Island** ahead. You should also be able to see from here whether or not the red flags are flying on the MoD's **Penally firing range**. If they are, you'll need to follow the detour inland on reaching the perimeter fence.

Before you reach the range though, you go through a gate and immediately lose the fence on your left — and the obvious path. Simply keep heading in the same direction, across the flat-topped cliff.

Caldey Island daytrips

Day visitors to Caldey Island are welcome, with boats leaving Tenby every 20 minutes during the summer. A small gift shop sells a variety of products made by the island's community of Cistercian monks. Visitors can explore the tiny island using official marked paths, or they can join a free, guided walk. The short chanted services that take place every day in the Abbey Church are also open to the public.

4 On reaching the edge of the range, if live firing is taking place, you'll need to use the alternative route described below. If, on the other hand, the range is open to the public, go through the gate and take the path to the right of the **sentry box**.

Trenches on the Penally range were used to train conscripts heading for the Western Front in World War One.

With Caldey Island straight ahead, go through several gates, heading out towards **Giltar Point**. Continue out to where the cliff path loops back on itself — just before a narrow trail heads out on to the rocky end of the headland opposite Caldey Island.

Caldey Island is home to a small community of Cistercian monks. They live in a grand, Italianate monastery, designed in the early twentieth century by John Coates Carter, one of the leading lights of the Arts and Crafts movement. South of the new buildings are the remains of the medieval Benedictine priory and St Illtyd's Church, with its leaning spire. The priory is thought to have been built on the site of a Celtic monastery, possibly dating back to the sixth century. A stone bearing inscriptions in both Latin and ancient Ogham, an early form of writing, was discovered in the priory grounds and is now on display in the church.

The route splits on several occasions as it encounters sandy hollows on this northern side of the headland. Keep right whenever possible. Go through a gate and descend a sandy path through the trees. Keep right at a fork, drop

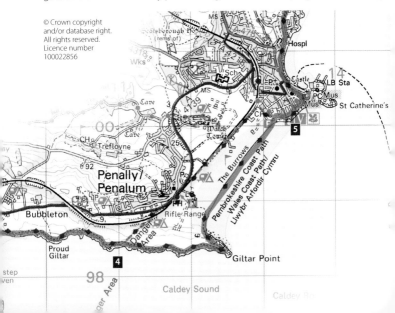

Sand, castle: *Tenby's South Beach with fortified St Catherine's Island just offshore*

to **South Beach** and then follow the line of sand dunes all the way to **Tenby** almost 2 kilometres away. The steps up from the beach lead up on to the **Esplanade**, along which you turn right. (If the tide is out, you may want to consider continuing along the sand, beneath the southern part of the town, towards **St Catherine's Island** and **Castle Hill**. There are several places here where you can access the town.)

Live-firing alternative: *Avoiding the military range*
If the range is closed to the public, the alternative route cuts about 650 metres off the total distance. Go through the gate and head downhill to the left, walking beside the fence. Go through the small gate in the fence at the base of slope and then under the railway. A track then leads to the **A4139** along which you turn right. There is a path off to the right, heading back to the coast, immediately after the station at **Penally**, but this cannot be used if firing is still taking place on the range. To continue on the alternative route, walk 500 metres beyond the station and then turn right along a gravel track. Pass to the right of a cottage and carefully cross the railway line to pick up a fenced path, which later broadens. At a crossing of ways, you could head right to reach the beach without running the gauntlet of the firing range, but the official route continues straight ahead, beside the railway.

Morning has broken: *First light illuminates the houses around Tenby's picturesque Old Harbour*

Bear right about 80 metres after passing the entrance to **Tenby Golf Club**. This path becomes a lane beside some cottages and continues uphill beside the **South Beach car park**. Where the lane swings left, take the path on the right. You'll soon see a path coming up from the beach. This is where the alternative route rejoins the main path.

5 Whether you've followed the **official route** across **South Beach** or the 'live-firing alternative' route, you now follow the **Esplanade** to the **old town wall of Tenby**.

On reaching the old town wall, follow the road left, but then go through the arch on the right, passing the **Imperial Hotel**. Swing right to continue along the seafront. Ignore the steps down into the harbour; instead swing left with the road. Take the narrow lane on the right and then turn left along the main shopping street.

Beyond the shops and restaurants, the road passes above **North Beach**. Take the next road on the right — **The Croft**. As the road swings up into a cul-de-sac, take the lane on the left, soon picking up a roadside path on the right. Where the lane ends, close to the entrance of **Meadow Farm**, you'll

see two paths continuing ahead. Take the one on the right, soon climbing concrete steps. At a path junction close to **Waterwynch Beach**, turn left.

6 Dropping to a lane, take the path opposite — through the trees. This is the first of several areas of **Hean Castle Estate** woodland passed between here and Saundersfoot. After the bridge, bear right. Emerging briefly from the trees via a gate, keep to the path at the base of the slope and then head

Tudor merchant's house

The 👁 **Merchant's House** in Tenby was built at the end of the fifteenth century — a time when the port and its traders were prospering. Managed by the National Trust, the oldest house in the town has been furnished to look as it did in 1500. The downstairs area consists of a shop — where the merchant would've sold products such as wool, vinegar and exotic spices — and a working kitchen. Visitors can see the family's home on the upper two storeys.

along another, shorter woodland trail. Walk with a fence on the right over **Rowston Hill**, but after that you're back out on the cliff again.

There are some good views back to Tenby from time to time, but it is to the next section of coast, the final few kilometres of the Pembrokeshire Coast Path, that your gaze will inevitably be drawn — when the thick vegetation allows. Those views improve considerably after the long, steep climb out of **Lodge Valley** and up to the gate near the **Coastguard lookout** at **Monkstone**. Cross the track here and continue following the fence on your right.

Before long, you reach a junction of paths in another area of **Hean Castle Estate woodland**. Go straight across, descending steeply at first. Turn left at a junction after a small bridge. The path winds its way downhill, past the fenced adit of a **disused iron ore mine**, to a junction above a beach. You'll see two paths heading uphill on the other side. Take the one on the right

Saundersfoot's pretty harbour

Fireworks reflected in the Old Harbour at Tenby

Tenby

The 'little fort of the fishes'

Tenby is an attractive town that has retained its charm and atmosphere despite being a popular holiday resort. Confined within medieval walls with several of its original gateways and towers still intact, the higher part of the settlement consists largely of a maze of narrow streets and alleyways. Brightly painted houses look down on the picturesque old harbour, protected by an island fortress, and vast, immaculate beaches lie to the north and south.

It started life as a fishing village. The Normans arrived at the end of the eleventh century and soon built fortifications on Castle Hill. What little remains of this early building has been incorporated into the excellent Tenby Museum. Some of the town's walled defences date from Norman times, and were reinforced during the fifteenth and sixteenth centuries when the threat of Spanish attack grew.

You could easily spend a day exploring Tenby: getting lost in its jumble of lanes and taking in some of its key attractions. As well as the main museum, a fifteenth-century townhouse on Quay Hill — the Tudor Merchant's House — has been opened to the public. Managed by the National Trust, it contains colourful wall hangings and Tudor-style furnishings.

More information: For an online guide to Tenby, visit www.tenbyvisitorguide.co.uk

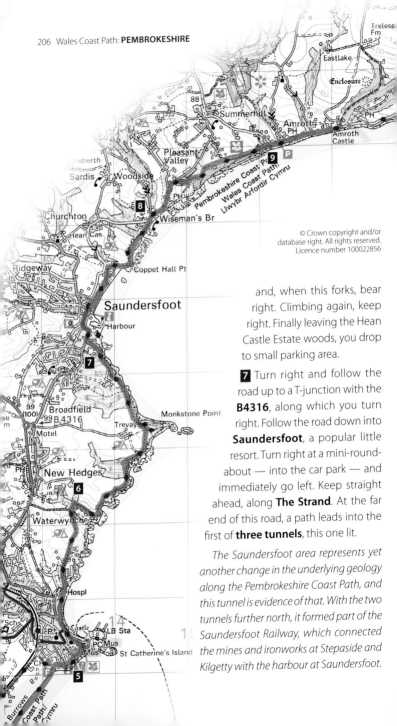

and, when this forks, bear right. Climbing again, keep right. Finally leaving the Hean Castle Estate woods, you drop to small parking area.

7 Turn right and follow the road up to a T-junction with the **B4316**, along which you turn right. Follow the road down into **Saundersfoot**, a popular little resort. Turn right at a mini-roundabout — into the car park — and immediately go left. Keep straight ahead, along **The Strand**. At the far end of this road, a path leads into the first of **three tunnels**, this one lit.

The Saundersfoot area represents yet another change in the underlying geology along the Pembrokeshire Coast Path, and this tunnel is evidence of that. With the two tunnels further north, it formed part of the Saundersfoot Railway, which connected the mines and ironworks at Stepaside and Kilgetty with the harbour at Saundersfoot.

Stop me and buy one: *Motorised ice cream sellers on the beach at Saundersfoot*

The coal measures here represent the youngest rocks along the coast, formed as the sea levels fell towards the end of the Carboniferous period, leaving vast areas of swamp. Coal had been dug in the area for several centuries, but it was only in the nineteenth century that mining and its associated industries really took off. Nearby deposits of haematite and reserves of limestone led to the rise of smelting and iron-working. The harbour at Saundersfoot flourished, and, by 1837, it had five jetties handling coal, iron ore, pig iron and brick, exporting to places as far away as Hong Kong.

The railway started life as a tramway, using horse-drawn vehicles. It was upgraded to a narrow-gauge railway in the 1870s, but the line closed for good in February 1939 after the collapse of the mining industry.

On the other side of this first tunnel, keep left, along the walkway and across the car park entrance at **Coppet Hall Point**. At the time of writing, there was a lot of building work going on here: plans were afoot to transform the car park and build a visitor centre with restaurant, public toilets, changing cubicles for bathers and outdoor activity centre. Swing right at the far end of the development, soon going through **another, shorter tunnel**.

The interesting, sloping rock formations on this beach were created by the power of the waves working on a fold in the coal measure.

The walkway, still following the line of the old tramway and railway, passes through the **third and longest tunnel** before continuing beside the beach to reach the road at **Wiseman's Bridge.**

During the summer of 1943, the beaches of Saundersfoot, Wiseman's Bridge and Amroth were the scene for full-scale rehearsals for the D-Day landings. Winston Churchill himself is said to have overseen part of the operations which involved as many as 100,000 men.

8 Turn right and follow the road past **Wiseman's Bridge Inn** and up to the left. About 120 metres beyond the road turning on the left for Pleasant Valley, take the dead-end lane on the right — **Cliff Road.** After the last of the cottages, a gate provides access to a surfaced path through trees and along the edge of farmland.

Watch for a gate on the right with coast path waymarkers on it. Go through this and turn left. The grassy path provides a welcome relief after all those kilometres of asphalt and concrete. Later, go left in the woods to descend the steps to the road at **Amroth**. You're nearly there now!

The long, sandy beach at Amroth

Submerged forest: *Five thousand year-old tree stumps are sometimes revealed on the beach at Amroth by low spring tides*

9 Turn right along the road. *At low tide, watch for tree stumps on the beach, the remains of an ancient woodland, long submerged by the sea.* After about 1 kilometre of roadside walking, passing the gateway to **Amroth Castle** on the way. Plaques next to the bridge and a sign pointing back to St Dogmael's, 300 kilometres away, herald your achievement in reaching the end of the Pembrokeshire Coast Path. It's time for a well-earned rest. Alternatively, you could just carry on along the Wales Coast Path... Only another 380 kilometres to go!

Welsh coastal place names

Welsh place names are as much a part of Wales's cultural distinctiveness as its mountains, sheep or rugged coast. To the English visitor, they may appear strangely foreign, confusing or simply unpronounceable. And yet, once carefully unravelled, they can tell us all sorts of fascinating things about a place — its landscape, character and history. Even these few common place name elements should help bring the Wales Coast Path alive.

Aber	river mouth, estuary	Ab-er
Afon	river	Av-on
Bad	ferry, boat	Bad
Bae	bay	Bai
Cae	field, enclosure	Kai
Carreg	stone, rock	Kar-reg
Cawl	sea kale	Kowl
Cei	quay	Kay
Cilfach	cove, creek	Kil-vakh
Clegyr	rock, cliff	Kleg-ir
Culfor	strait	Kil-vor
Din/dinas	citadel; hillfort; fortified hill	Deen/Deen-as
Dwr/dwfr	water	Doer/Doo-vr
Dyffryn	valley; bottom	Duff-ryn
Eglwys	church	Eg-looees

The vast surfer's beach at Freshwater West

Ffynnon	well; spring; fountain; source	*Fun-on*
Goleudy	lighthouse	*Gol-ay-dee*
Glan	shore	*Glan*
Gwymon	seaweed	*Gwi-mon*
Harbwr	harbour	*Haboor*
Heli	salt water, brine	*Hel-lee*
Llech	flat stone, flagstone, slate	*Th-lekh*
Maen	stone; standing stone	*Mine*
Mor	sea, ocean	*More*
Morfa	sea marsh, salt marsh	*Mor-va*
Moryd	estuary, channel	*Mor-rid*
Ogof	cave	*Og-ov*
Parrog	flat land by the sea	*Par-rog*
Penrhyn	headland	*Pen-rin*
Pigyn	point	*Pig-in*
Pont/bont	bridge, arch	*Pont/Bont*
Porth	harbour	*Porth*
Pwll	pool, pit	*Pooth*
Tafol	dock	*Tav-ol*
Ton/don	wave	*Ton/Don*
Traeth	beach	*Treye-th*
Trwyn	nose; point, cape	*Troo-een*
Tywyn	sandy shore sand dunes	*Tow-in*
Ynys	island	*Un-iss*

"*Wales, where the past still lives. Where every place has its tradition, every name its poetry ...*"

Matthew Arnold *On the Study of Celtic Literature*, 1866

Visitor Information

Wales Coast Path

Comprehensive information about all sections of the Wales Coast Path can be found on the official website at **www.walescoastpath.gov.uk** and **www.walescoastpath.co.uk**

'Visit Wales'

The Visit Wales website covers everything from accommodation to attractions. For information on the area covered by this book, see **www.visitwales. com/explore/west-wales/pembrokeshire**

Pembrokeshire

For local information, from what to do to eating out, see **www.visitpembrokeshire.com.** For information specifically about the National Park, see **www. pembrokeshirecoast.org.uk**

Tourist Information Centres

Pembrokeshire's main TICs provide free information on everything from accommodation and travel to what's on and walking advice.

Newport	01239 820912	newporttic@pembrokeshirecoast.org.uk
Fishguard	01437 776636	fishguard.tic@pembrokeshire.gov.uk
St Davids	01437 720392	info@orielyparc.co.uk
Milford Haven	01437 771818	milford.tic@pembrokeshire.gov.uk
Pembroke	01437 776499	pembroke.tic@pembrokeshire.gov.uk
Tenby	01834 842402	tenby.tic@pembrokeshire.gov.uk

Where to stay

There's lots of accommodation close to the Wales Coast Path in Pembrokeshire, from campsites, youth hostels and B&Bs to holiday cottages and hotels. Tourist Information Centre staff will know what's available locally and can even book for you. Alternatively, book online. Find campsites at **www. ukcampsite.co.uk**

Luggage Carrying Service

For relatively inexpensive, door-to-door luggage transfer between overnight stops: 'Luggage Transfers', 01437 723 030 | **www.luggagetransfers.co.uk**

Walking holidays

Several companies offer complete walking packages including: accommodation, local information, maps, baggage transfer and transport.

Celtic Trails   01291 689774 | **www.celtic-trails.com** | info@celtic-trails.com

Contours   01629 821900 | **www.contours.co.uk** | info@contours.co.uk

Mickledore   01768772335|**www.mickledore.co.uk**|info@mickledore.co.uk

Train and buses

For public transport information across Wales, see Traveline Cymru. 0871 200 22 33 | **www.traveline-cymru.info**

Fishguard, Milford Haven, Pembroke Dock, Haverfordwest and Tenby are all served by reasonably regular train services. All rail services in Wales are run by Arriva Trains Wales. For more information on timetables and fares, visit www.arrivatrainswales.co.uk or National Rail Enquiries www.nationalrail.co.uk. There are regular bus services throughout the county, and five coastal bus services covering most of the National Trail. These handy little walkers' buses run seven days a week throughout the summer. For more information, see **www.pembrokeshire.gov.uk**

Taxis

Cardigan: Robins Taxi | 01239 612190

Fishguard: Carrots Cabs | 01348 872088 | **www.carrotscabs.co.uk** | info@carrotscabs.co.uk

St Davids: Tony's Taxis | 01437 720931 | **www.tonystaxis.net** | tonys.taxis@btopenworld.com

Milford Haven: Jock's Taxis | 01646 698818

Pembroke: Castle Cars | 01646 622440

Tenby: Tenby Taxis | 01834 843678 | **www.tenbytaxis.com**

Cycle hire

Carningli Bike Hire. Mountain bikes and hybrids for all ages. Carningli Centre, East Street, Newport | 01239 820724 | www.carninglibikehire.com | info@carningli.co.uk

Mike's Bikes. Can deliver direct to accommodation. 17 Prendergast, Haverfordwest | 01437 760068 | www.mikes-bikes.co.uk | info@mikes-bikes.co.uk

Cycle repairs

Mike's Bikes (see above) also carries out bike repairs as does Tenby Cycles, 16A The Norton, Tenby | 01834 845573 | www.tenbycycles.co.uk | contactus@tenbycycles.co.uk

Boat Trips

Ramsey Island. All-day trip from St Justinian's, including guided walk led by RSPB warden. April 1 to October 31. Thousand Islands Expeditions, Cross Square, St Davids | 01437 721721 | **www.thousandislands.co.uk**

Skomer. The island is open to the public from April 1 (or Good Friday, whichever is earlier) to September 30. Closed Mondays, except bank holidays. Boats depart from Martin's Haven at 10am, 11am and 12pm; return from 3pm onwards. 01646 636800 | **www.welshwildlife.org**

Caldey Island. From Easter until October 31, boats run daily (except Sunday) every 30 minutes from 10.30am. Tickets from booth at Tenby Harbour | 01834 844453 | **www.caldey-island.co.uk** | inquiries@caldey-island.co.uk

Military ranges

The MoD's Castlemartin range is divided in two: Range West and Range East. The Pembrokeshire Coast Path passes through the latter, which is closed to the public during live firing. To check firing times, phone 01646 662367 or see **www.gov.uk/government/publications/castlemartin-firing-notice--2** Information on the Penally rifle range can be obtained by ringing the automated service 01834 845950 or the administrative officer on 01834 843522

Emergencies

In an emergency, call 999 or 112 and ask for the service your require: Ambulance, Police, Fire or Coastguard. North Wales police 01286 673347.

Tides

Short stretches of the Pembrokeshire Coast Path are only accessible for a short period either side of low tide. To avoid long inland detours, check tide times before you go. Tide table booklets are widely available from TICs and local shops for about £1. Tide tables for the full year are also published online at **www.visitpembrokeshire.com**

Weather forecasts

For reliable, up-to-date weather forecasts, see **www.bbc.co.uk/weather** or **www.metoffice.gov.uk/weather/uk.**

Annual events

Fishguard Folk Festival: Late May bank holiday weekend | **www.pembrokeshire-folk-music.co.uk**

St Davids Cathedral Festival: nine-day classical music festival, May/June | **www.stdavidscathedralfestival.co.uk**

Fishguard International Music Festival: July | **www.fishguardmusicfestival.co.uk**

Wales Coast Path: Official Guides

The **Official Guides** to the **Wales Coast Path** are endorsed by Natural Resources Wales, the Welsh government body which developed and manages the path. The guides break the Wales Coast Path into seven main sections, giving both long-distance and local walkers everything they need to enjoy all 870 miles of this world-class route.

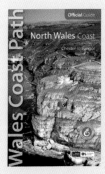

North Wales Coast
Chester to Bangor
ISBN: 978-0-9559625-1-6

Isle of Anglesey
Circuit from Menai Bridge
ISBN: 978-1-902512-15-0

Llŷn Peninsula
Bangor to Porthmadog
ISBN: 978-1-908632-24-1

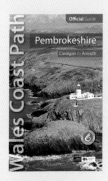

Pembrokeshire
Cardigan to Amroth
ISBN: 978-1-908632-23-4

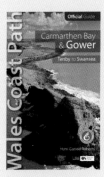

Carmarthen Bay &
Gower *Tenby to Swansea*
ISBN: 978-1-908632-26-5

South Wales Coast
Swansea to Chepstow
ISBN: 978-1-908632-27-2

Wales Coast Path: Top 10 Walks

Award-winning pocket-size walking guides to the most popular, easy circular walks along key sections of the Wales Coast Path. The full series will cover the whole path in ten attractive guides.

Currently available

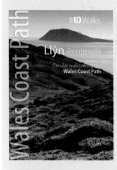

Top 10 Walks:
Llyn Peninsula
ISBN: 978-1-902512-34-1

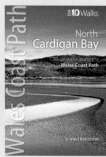

Top 10 Walks:
Cardigan Bay North
ISBN: 978-1 908632-13-5

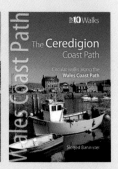

Top 10 Walks:
The Ceredigion Coast
ISBN: 978-1-908632-28-9

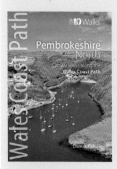

Top 10 Walks:
Pembrokeshire North
ISBN: 978-1-908632-29-6

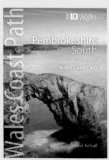

Top 10 Walks:
Pembrokeshire South
ISBN: 978-1 908632-30-2

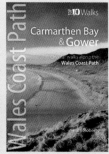

Top 10 Walks:
Carmarthenshire & Gower
ISBN: 978-1-908632-16-6